EMOTIONAL INTELLIGENCE COLLECTION 2-IN-1 BUNDLE

Emotional Intelligence
+
Cognitive Behavioral Therapy (CBT) - The #1 Complete Box Set to Understand Your Emotions and Reshape Your Brain

EMOTIONAL INTELLIGENCE:

Understand Your Emotions and Create Profound Relationships

Discover How to Develop Emotional Awareness, EQ, and Social Intelligence, Even if You're a Clueless Beginner

Table of Contents

Introduction 5
Chapter 1: What is Emotional Intelligence? 7
Chapter 2: Emotional Intelligence in Daily Life 17
Chapter 3: Building Self-Awareness Skills 28
Chapter 4: Building Self-Management Skills 46
Chapter 5: Building Social Awareness Skills 59
Chapter 6: Building Relationship Management Skills 68
Conclusion 95

Congratulations on purchasing *Emotional intelligence 2.0: A Practical Guide for Beginners* and thank you for doing so. Every effort was made to ensure it is full of as much useful information as possible. Please enjoy!

Introduction

You have heard so much about emotional intelligence that your interest is piqued. Whether you are a top-management official at work or a stay-at-home mom, emotional intelligence is important in your life. I commend you for taking the steps to develop your emotional intelligence skills. By doing so, you will only improve your quality of life from how you feel about yourself to how you feel about others, and ultimately, how others feel about you.

The following chapters will discuss how you can develop your ability to master emotional intelligence and to see great improvements in your personal and professional life. The book is divided into 6 easy-to-read chapters that will give you insight into how to manage your emotional intelligence.

The first chapter will give a brief overview of what emotional intelligence is. Then the subsequent chapters will break down the tenets of emotional intelligence into more detail. Chapter 2 builds on Chapter 1 and explores what emotional intelligence looks like in your everyday life. From this chapter, we dive right into building skills that will help you improve your emotional intelligence. In Chapter 3, how to manage your emotions will be discussed, followed by how to improve your self-awareness in Chapter 4. Chapter 5 explains how to use social awareness and relationship management respectively.

At the end of every chapter, there will be a special section dedicated to giving you skills on how to develop each skill in order to become better at emotional intelligence. Also, please note that throughout the chapters, you will learn about Valerie who does not have an idea about emotional intelligence and her socially bankrupt life reflects it. Please do not be like Valerie!

Hopefully, by the end of this book, you will learn a lot from Valerie on what to do and what not to do in regards to emotional intelligence. At the end of the chapter, bullet points of the chapter topics and activities you can do to help develop your emotional intelligence will be given. Take small baby steps and do not be afraid to feel awkward as you try to implement the changes associated with emotional intelligence into your life. Every journey must start with one step and it is difficult before it gets easier. By the time you finish, you will notice how much your life has improved just because you decided to take the step to be more emotionally intelligent.

There are plenty of books on this subject on the market, so thanks again for choosing this one! Every effort was made to ensure it is full of as much useful information as possible. Please enjoy!

Chapter 1: What is Emotional Intelligence?

Meet Valerie. Valerie is a typical American who is married with two kids, a house, and a white picket fence. Oh yeah, she has a beautiful black Labrador as well. Valerie would consider her to have an average level of emotional intelligence. She does ok at work. Her familial, personal, and professional relationships are so-so. She feels like she's walking through life. Not going fast or slow, but just regular shmegular. She doesn't always feel in control and sometimes has panic attacks because she is overwhelmed, stressed, and unhealthy. She figures everyone else is going through the same things so it is not a big problem.

Cut to one busy day where Valerie is rushing to work because she has not communicated to her family members that she needs help and all of the chores and housework falls on her. Not too mention, she had to stay late at work the night before because she is a people pleaser which made her oversleep in the first place. Picture Valerie in a car, speeding down the highway in the rain before she hydroplanes smack dab into an eighteen-wheeler. Her car spins out of control and Valerie finds herself pinned behind her steering wheel in her car that is sideways in a ditch. Of course, a Good Samaritan saw the incident and immediately called emergency services who rushed to the scene. After the paramedics help her out the car, she is whisked to the hospital.

The good news is, she was alive. The bad news is, she has amnesia and she has to learn everything all over again. Facts like her children's names, her husband's name, and her dog's name will be seemingly easy to learn. However, the nuances of emotional intelligence seemed much more difficult to learn. She has to learn how to identify her personal emotions, manage them when reacting to other people, as well as managing her social settings and relationships. Whew! Valerie is on a quest to relearn what emotional intelligence is, but Valerie is not alone. There are a lot of people who want to learn how to be emotionally intelligent and are on the same path as Valerie.

This book attempts to help people like Valerie and the readers navigate the tricky, topsy-turvy, abstract world of emotions and the unspoken rules that come with it. Unlike Valerie who is starting with a blank slate, most people have some type of experience with their emotions whether they have anger issues, are people pleasers, or are narcissists. Emotional intelligence draws upon your personal preferences and experiences to figure out how to survive in the world. In order to improve upon one's emotional intelligence, one must first understand what emotional intelligence is.

So what is emotional intelligence? Known in short as EI, emotional intelligence is the multi-faceted capacity of being in tune with your personal thoughts and emotions and being able to manage them in your daily living and in your dealings with other people. In order to be emotionally intelligent, you must first have mastery of who you are and know how to handle your emotions. Then you must know how to navigate relationships with other people, especially how to interpret and understand their emotions and how to be savvy in the way you respond to their emotions for optimal results. In other words, to be emotionally intelligent, you need to know what to say, when to say it, and how to say it. Sounds like a lot? You're right. Becoming emotionally intelligent can be overwhelming, but it is not impossible. It is a skill that can be learned with practice.

Being emotionally intelligent is a trait many want to acquire because research has shown that emotionally intelligent people are deemed better leaders, better friends, and better family members. People with emotional intelligence do not necessarily have the highest IQ, but they understand how people work. As a result, their acumen in dealing with people helps them to be successful in a way that people who are not emotionally intelligent are not able to achieve.

Emotional intelligence was brought to the mainstream in 1995 by Daniel Goleman when he wrote the book *Emotional Intelligence: Why It Can Matter More Than IQ*. This book was seminal in changing how people thought about the power of emotions. Before this book, emotions were not seen as powerful tools to help you succeed. Emotions were seen as a hindrance. Goldman brought the importance of being emotionally intelligent to the forefront, but it was not an idea that originated with him. Way back in the day, over 2,000 years ago, Plato wrote that "All learning has an emotional base." Even though Plato had said that emotions were important centuries earlier, scientists did not always see it that way. However, in the 1920s, the idea that emotions were important re-emerged when Edward Thorndike named the ability to get along with others as "social intelligence."

In 1950, Abraham Maslow sparked the human potential movement and wrote about the importance of people enhancing their mental, physical, emotional, and spiritual strengths. From his research, lots of similar movements were launched and people began to build on his ideas. From this birth of new knowledge, two researchers, Peter Salovey and John "Jack" Mayer in the 1990s, have been credited with first using the term 'emotional intelligence.' In the article, Salovey and Mayer defined emotional intelligence as scientifically testable "intelligence." This work set the foundation for Daniel Goleman's book in 1995. From there, many different offshoots of emotional intelligence were developed. For the purpose of this book, we will focus on emotional intelligence as being composed of four different parts consisting of self-management, self-awareness, social awareness, and relationship management.

Self-awareness is being in tune with your emotions. If you are self-aware, you are great at identifying and deciphering your emotions and using them effectively when you react to a situation. Self-management is the act of managing your emotions and the reactions to any situation you may find yourself in. The word 'manage' is key in the definition of self-management. If you are great at self-management, it does not mean that you do not get angry or experience emotions at all. It means that you are adept at how you manage those emotions to get the outcome you want. Social awareness is being keen to the social environment around you. And relationship management is all about handling your relationships whether they be professional, personal, or even the relationship with yourself. In later chapters, each separate component will be delved into in greater detail.

To understand how one learns about emotional intelligence, a person must understand how our brains work. Our brain is divided into three separate parts — the basal ganglia, limbic system, and neocortex. The basal ganglia are at the root of our brain and it is considered the place where all our instincts reside. When you feel something in your gut, the information travels directly to this region of your brain without going through the other regions. This is information that you do not have to think about at all. The next part of the brain is the limbic system. The information processed by this part of your brain is considered to be processed on the subconscious level. Subconscious level information is a step above unconscious information and that information is right below our level of awareness. The subconscious level is where our emotions reside. It stores information about experiences good and bad that affect our behaviors, as well as it stores our value judgments. The neocortex is the next part of the brain. It controls your level of awareness. The information in this part of the brain is able to be accessed at will. It controls our reasoning, language, and thoughts. This brief overview of the brain is helpful to understand because certain activities suggested later on in the book target certain aspects of the brain. It is a cool tidbit to understand how the activities strengthen certain aspects of your brain so you can learn how to control your emotional intelligence better and be more aware.

Emotionally Intelligent Character Traits

How does someone who is emotionally intelligent act? People who are emotionally intelligent normally have a few characteristics that let others know they are emotionally intelligent individuals.

- Emotionally intelligent people have empathy. They are able to understand how others are feeling in any given situation. In other words, like the cliché says, emotionally intelligent people are able to walk in someone else's shoes. They are able to understand how someone with a sick child may be having a rough time or understand the importance of being nice to everyone whether they have experienced that situation or not.

- Emotional intelligent people also think deeply about their emotions and other people's emotions – a lot. They are pros at knowing how to relate and manipulate to other people in order to get the best outcome possible.

- Emotionally intelligent people do not run from criticism. They are able to take feedback easily without being defensive. They are able to take what people say about them, dissect the criticism, and take from the criticism what they may.

- Emotionally intelligent people are also genuine people. They seek authenticity in their relationships with other people and tend to see the best in people. Hence, they also are able to forgive and forget slights against them rather easily.

- People who are emotionally intelligent are very positive. They are not angels. However, they are effective at refocusing their thoughts, so they do not act impulsively and do something that they will regret later.

- Emotionally intelligent people do not run from confrontation. They face the criticism head-on and then go from there. They handle the conflict with ease, even if their egos are wounded in the process.

- Emotionally intelligent people are excellent communicators. They know their personality type and communication style and are able to effectively communicate with others and know the style in which they prefer to be communicated.

People who are not emotionally intelligent tend to be the exact opposite.

- They are easily flustered and easily angered.

- They are selfish and they only care about one person - themselves.

- They do not think before they speak and they talk all the time without any care to how other people may react to what they are saying.

- People who are not emotionally intelligent are usually not the easiest people to get along with.

Emotionally intelligent people are leagues ahead of people who are not emotionally intelligent. Interestingly, one can have characteristics of being emotionally intelligent and also have characteristics of not being emotionally intelligent. The key is to try and work on your emotional intelligence until you are competent in all four areas of being emotionally intelligent. This takes work.

For someone who has never ever thought about learning more about emotional intelligence, the information explained thus far may seem suspect. You may be one of the people who believe that emotional intelligence is a fluke. You may think that it is not necessary or important to be in tune with your emotions or in tune with the emotions of others in order to be a better person. You may think emotional intelligence is nothing but hippy-dippy foolery that has no place in the same sentence with rational thought. You may think that emotional intelligence has no effect on your success. However, think of that one person that you would not rather be around. This person always makes inappropriate jokes. They never know what to say. It is like they always have a foot in their mouth. These types of people have no self-awareness. No one wants to be around them. This is why emotional intelligence matters. There is no black-and-white version of emotional intelligence.

It is possible that you are good with some of the aspects of emotional intelligence and you need help controlling the other aspects. Perhaps you are good at knowing your feelings and you're able to manage your emotions, but you are terrible at communicating with others. Hence, your relationship management needs work. Perhaps you are excellent at navigating relations and social settings, whether they are professional or personal because you are great at putting on a front but your personal life is in shambles. You may need to work on your self-awareness. Or perhaps, you can easily be wonderful at managing other people's relationships. You can be the one friend that everyone comes to when they need help, but you are horrible at your own self-management. It happens. Just because you are okay with three out of the four aspects of emotional intelligence does not mean that you cannot improve the other aspects. Wanting to be aware of how emotional intelligence works is commendable and there are definitely skills and exercises that you can do to improve each and every aspect of your emotional intelligence core.

Yet, emotional intelligence can have a dark side. There are some people who are master manipulators. They are so good at emotional intelligence that they can draw upon what someone else is feeling in order to get the outcome that they want. These people know how to pit people against each other, play the victim, and play on people's emotions to remain in control at all times. If you are not emotionally intelligent, you can really fall victim to their traps rather quickly. One of the most important reasons for developing your emotional intelligence is to be a better person and to protect yourself against people who have nefarious intentions.

Lucky for Valerie, she is starting with a blank slate when learning how to develop her emotional intelligence. She does not have to be concerned about all the baggage that comes with learning a new skill. For her, she has to begin by learning what emotional intelligence is. So buckle up. The next chapter will go into more detail about how emotional intelligence affects our daily life whether we are aware of it or not.

Chapter Highlights

- Emotional intelligence was coined by Daniel Goleman in 1995 by his book *Emotional Intelligence: Why It Is More Important Than Your IQ*.
- Emotional Intelligence is composed of four different parts — self-management, self-awareness, social awareness, and relationship management.
- Our brain is composed of three regions that control our thoughts and emotions. By doing exercises to improve every aspect of our brain, one can improve their emotional intelligence.

Do the Work

- Why are you interested in learning more about emotional intelligence? Is it to improve personally or is it to improve in a professional setting or is it another reason? Knowing why you want to learn about emotional intelligence can help you when you get to a difficult spot in your learning.
- Do you think that you have more traits of being emotionally intelligent or more traits of not being emotionally intelligent?
- Emotional intelligence is composed of four different components — self-awareness, self-management, social

awareness, and relationship management. Which component do you think you need to work on?
- Before emotional intelligence was brought to the forefront, there was a philosopher who said that "emotions are at the base of every decision?" Who was it?

Chapter 2: Emotional Intelligence in Daily Life

Remember Valerie? Yeah, things have not been going as smoothly for her ever since she's gotten home from the hospital. She has relearned basic traits such as eating and going to the restroom, but she has not discovered how to completely control her emotions yet. Her therapist keeps telling her that she needs to look into it, but she has no idea where to begin. The more she learned, she discovered that emotional intelligence is way more important in her life than she expected. Just like Valerie, emotional intelligence has a place in every person's life. However, she knows that she has a long road ahead of her.

Emotional intelligence helps our relationships with others. Emotional intelligence helps us be happier with ourselves and it helps people move throughout life a whole lot easier than if they didn't have emotional intelligence. Research has evolved to show that emotional intelligence has a place in every aspect of our life as well from the workplace to your mental and physical health to your family and social environment. While there are specific ways to improve one's emotional intelligence by focusing on the component of emotional intelligence that they are not as healthy in, there are a few general suggestions to help one improve their emotional intelligence.

One major suggestion is to expand the vocabulary that describes your emotions. When you say someone is happy, what version of happy are they? Are they ecstatic, mellow, or jumping with joy? When someone is mad, are they livid, disappointed, or upset? If you need help developing your emotional vocabulary, you can start by learning a new emotional word daily by going to the dictionary. You can even learn foreign words to help with your task. The more vocabulary you have to describe how you are feeling and how others are feeling helps your brain react to emotional situations better.

Emotional intelligence can be tricky because a person can hide the emotions that they are feeling. If you expect all people to cry when they are sad, a person who is sad and does not cry and laughs instead will throw you off guard. How about if a person is happy and cries for joy instead of smiling and laughing when they are happy? People who react to their emotions in a non-stereotypical way can cause you issues when trying to figure out how to react to their emotions. On the other hand, there are tons of people who are pros at hiding their true emotions. Someone can be boiling on the inside, but outwardly say that they are happy. If people are able to lie about how they feel or act in ways that always truly depict how they feel, how in the world are you able to determine the best response of responding to people?

Research points to a new way of understanding how our brain works which in turn will help us understand how to be better at being emotionally intelligent. We already know that our brain has three different parts that help determine your emotions and controls how to react to your emotions and the emotional responses of others. Researchers have now figured out that our brain works from an encyclopedia of experiences that we have. The more information we have in our brain's encyclopedia and the varied emotions we can draw from, the better reactions our brain can pull out from its encyclopedia of emotional responses in order to determine what is the best way to react to any given situation. (This is why understanding the different degrees of emotions by improving your emotional vocabulary are important.) Research has helped us to understand that even though people sometimes say one thing, their face gives away their true emotions. Maybe they are smiling but they have a slight scowl which points to their true displeasure. Maybe they are smiling but their eyes have sadness about them or their smile doesn't include their eyes. Understanding the nuances of emotions helps someone draw quickly and correctly from their brain's encyclopedia. This ability to break down emotions and their nuances are called emotional granularity. This is an important tool to have in your emotional intelligence toolkit.

Self-awareness is an important aspect of emotional intelligence in our day-to-day living. Since emotional intelligence is layered, this would be the first layer to master. Self-aware people are able to identify and understand their emotions quickly. A key benefit of being self-aware is knowing when you are engaging in toxic behavior or even engaging in overly happy behavior that can cause issues as well. When they are able to identify these emotions, then they are able to properly choose how to manage those emotions. For example, stress is a common issue that many people have to deal with. Research has shown that stress is a common denominator in certain chronic illness like heart diseases, high blood pressure, and obesity to name a few. However, emotionally intelligent people are able to deal with it easier and sustain themselves in stressful situations in a way that people who are not emotionally intelligent are unable to. For example, an emotionally intelligent person is able to quickly identify what stresses them out and then choose the proper response to that trigger. This is what self-management is. Knowing how to respond to any given situation and it is the second layer of emotional intelligence. When you are emotionally intelligent, you are able to properly de-escalate the situation when you are feeling stressed whether that is to alter your surroundings or properly handle your responses to other people. In some instances, stress is unavoidable especially if certain relationships you have bring on stress. Emotionally intelligent people find amazing ways to handle the stress to prevent a mental health breakdown. At times, a professional must be sought when dealing with stress and its impact on your life. That's totally ok. The key to being self-aware is the action part of the definition when you decide to do something about the emotions you are facing. (Remember, non-action is also a form of action.) Many people can identify issues they may have, but choose to do nothing about it or continue in the same destructive cycles. Self-aware people and those who practice self-management are able to manage the situation and come out stronger than before.

For Valerie, to improve her emotional intelligence, she has to rebuild her emotional encyclopedia so she has experiences to draw from. After the wreck, she spent lots of time at home recovering. She got to learn her family better and engaged with many health professionals that helped with her recovery. She also discovered Google which is an amazing tool that she has been using to develop her emotional intelligence. During this time, she was able to learn what types of things that made her happy and what made her upset. She noticed that having breakfast in bed delivered to her made her happy. She noticed that when her children did what she wanted them to do, that made her happy. On the other side, when the nurses made her take medicine she did not want, she did not like it. Initially, she realized that throwing a tantrum like a toddler did not help. She had to manage the emotion in a different way. She realized that she could express her displeasure in a different way. She could state that she did not like taking the medication, but would still take it. The key to remember from this example is that communication is the key when you are managing the emotions that you may have. Oftentimes, identifying the emotion is the easy part. The difficult part of being emotionally intelligent happens when you have to manage those emotions. And for many people, communication is especially difficult when you have to explain unpleasant things to people. However, emotionally intelligent person expressed how they feel and then take the action. Valerie realized that while she did not like taking her medicine, she would have to in order to get well. So the response she deemed appropriate to this situation was to express her displeasure while taking the medicine since it was necessary.

Social awareness is the next aspect of emotional intelligence that affects us in our day-to-day life. It is the third layer to master. The social setting in which you find yourself plays a role in how you handle yourself. You know the saying, "There's a time and place for everything?" It is true. Social awareness is summed up neatly in that saying. A person is going to act differently at home than they would at work versus how they would act in a religious setting or a social setting like a bar or club. To master social awareness, you have to pick up quickly on what type of setting you are in. Is it formal or more relaxed? Is it professional or is it casual? One way to figure that out if you have no idea is to look at what other people are doing. How are they dressed? Are they wearing skimpy clothes or suits and dresses? How are they talking? Are they talking loudly, normally, or are they being quiet? What kind of language are they using? Are they using profanity or are they using vernacular or academic language? To understand how to act properly, you can also look at how others are acting in the situation. Are they being loud? Or only a few people are being loud? Then notice how other people are reacting to them. Noticing how people act and how others react to their actions is a big clue on how to be socially aware. Are people who wear certain clothes acting a certain way or are they being outcasted? The key to mastering being socially aware is to become observant and notice what is going on around you. A trick that some people use no matter what social setting they are in is to be quiet, sit in a corner and watch what is going on. Socially aware people sometimes take people that they trust to the side to ask questions about social settings they may find themselves in. On the flip side, you have to be true in situations no matter what others are doing, even if it is deemed socially acceptable. For example, have you ever found yourself in a situation where it was ok to bully and make fun of other people? That's not a nice thing, but if you don't bully the other person, then people would be bullying you. Emotionally intelligent people are able to stand for their beliefs even when it is unfavorable.

Valerie had to quickly realize that social settings dictate her reactions. After taking the medicine she did not like, she has been approved to go back to her former job. She works as a customer service representative at a technology company that manufactures the latest software. Before she was involved in her accident, she was a top customer service rep. After going through a two-week training, her love for technology has come back. She is a pro at understanding the technology, but understanding how to deal with other people in a work setting is proving to be a challenge. First, Valerie has to deal with the customers. Next, she has to deal with her co-workers and then she has to deal with her managers and supervisors. She notices that the company is pretty relaxed. She does not have to dress up for work. Valerie is able to pick up on the playful banter amongst her co-workers and managers that make her feel more relaxed. The company also plays music in the background to help deal with the stress.

Everything was going well until Valerie has to deal with a very angry customer on a call. Flabbergasted, she is immediately quiet. She notices that the person right beside her seems to be on a stressful call and they are biting the top of their pen vigorously. Valerie has no idea how to respond. Her initial thought is to yell at the customer and hang up, but last week, she saw someone do that and that co-worker lost their job. The longer she waits on how to respond to the customer, she notices that the person's voice continues to rise. Valerie feels her heartbeat racing and she knows that getting yelled at is a stress trigger of hers. She looks around and notices that her co-worker begins to smile and talk with their difficult customer so she thinks she will try that. Valerie begins to smile and notices immediately that her heartbeat slows down. She talks slowly and begins to give the customer options on how to resolve the conflict. She notices that her co-workers are doing similar techniques. She begins to relax and the customer decides that she would like to speak with a manager. Valerie immediately transfers the call to a manager. Valerie was able to handle her social setting by observing what others were doing and making notes of examples of what she had seen before. In this came, the old adage "When in Rome, do as the Romans do" saved her. After that one incident, Valerie was able to continue being relaxed, yet professional in her work setting.

Relationship management is the last key component that we have to deal with in our daily life and it is the last component of emotional intelligence. Relationships are everywhere! Our relationship with our self is of utmost importance, but our relationships with others are just as important. Emotionally intelligent people know how to react to a situation based on the relationship they have with someone. A relationship with a homeless stranger on the street will be different from your spouse versus the relationship with your teenager or toddler.

Knowing the dynamics of every relationship is very important. Most people have a baseline of respect and kindness for everyone they meet. This could also be described as common courtesy. But emotionally intelligent people understand the nuances of relationships, and when necessary, they can manipulate a relationship to get the results that they want. In this case, manipulation is not being defined as a negative, but as an action that emotionally intelligent people know how to use to navigate situations in their daily life. People who use manipulation to control people for nefarious gains are different from people who use manipulation to get the results that they want. Evil manipulators tend to cause destruction in their relationships, whereas, emotionally intelligent people are able to maintain their relationships and they are able to return the favor of scratching others back when necessary.

An often understated, important aspect of being an emotionally intelligent being is the importance of knowing how to manage your time. Time-management is a crucial foundation that emotional intelligence rests on. Have you ever noticed how calm people who always have it together seem to be? They do not ever seem frazzled and their hair always seems to be done? Well, time management is a tool I'm sure they are using. Just like emotional intelligence, time management is a skill that can be learned. Later on in the book, we will take a look at how important time management is and work on an activity to evaluate your time management.

Our friend Valerie is noticing that there is a difference in the way that her co-workers treat her versus her husband and her children. One thing she has noticed is that they know how to manage their situation to get optimal results. As a working mom, she is having a difficult time managing her responsibilities at home. On one hand, she has to handle her responsibilities at her job and on the other hand, she has to handle her cooking, cleaning, and personal maintenance too. She feels like there is not enough time in the day. She feels like her mind is racing all the time and she is having small panic attacks. She has no idea what to do except to ask for help from the different relationships that she has.

Valerie first had a sit down with her husband to see if he wouldn't mind ordering take out or preparing food for the kids once or twice a week to see if she could get some me time. Because Valerie quickly realized that the best time to ask her husband about something is after she serves him her famous lemon meringue pie, she asked him right after he ate a piece. Of course, he happily agreed. The next task she knew she needed to accomplish was to get her children, a teenager and toddler, to take more responsibility in the household. Instead of whining to her children, she knew the dynamics of the relationship and she was able to use humor to address the issue. Her children happily agreed. The stress from trying to do everything herself had begun to pack on the pounds. So she began to meditate, exercise, communicate better, and clear out her schedule. Valerie realized that reaching out to the relationships that she had and communicating her feelings and how they can make the best out of the relationship was important. Valerie felt super accomplished!

Things were going well for a week until everything went back to the way they were. Valerie no longer had time to exercise or relax. She went back to scrambling to do everything. One night, she hears a ring at the doorbell. It is Patty, the interim replacement to her neighborhood association who wanted to know when Valerie could take her position back. Valerie has a tumble of emotions and she is not sure how to react so she told Patty she would think about it.

As you can see, Valerie thought that she had everything figured out, but soon learned that the journey to emotional intelligence is never over. You are always learning and developing your emotional intelligence. Some days are better than others and some days are total, utter failures. Valerie's life feels quite chaotic again and she needs the tools of emotional intelligence to learn how to navigate. In order to do so, she must first learn how to be in touch with her emotions. She must learn how to thoroughly dissect what her emotions mean and that is the subject of the next chapter of the book.

Chapter Highlights

- Emotional granularity is paramount in helping you pick out a wide range of emotions to choose from. The wider your emotional vocabulary, whether the words come from foreign languages or your native language, the better you are able to create an encyclopedia in which your brain can draw from when trying to figure out what is the proper reaction to any situation.
- There are different tools you can use to prepare yourself with emotional intelligence such as meditation, exercise, and communication.
- Self-awareness, self-management, social awareness, and relationship all play a major role in our day-to-day life.

Do the Work

- Make a commitment to find words to describe emotional situations that you find yourself in. Try to pepper your language with a few foreign words to give your emotional vocabulary and encyclopedia more nuance.

- How would you rate your level of communication on a scale of 1 to 10? Be honest with yourself.
- What are some initial thoughts you have on how you can improve your communication?
- How are you currently handling your time management? Is there anything you can get rid of?
- If you were Valerie, what would be your initial response when speaking with Patty? What do you think would be the best response for responding to Patty?

Chapter 3: Building Self-Awareness Skills

Valerie often has weird sensations. She has learned that these weird sensations are called emotions. She has developed a basic emotional intelligence encyclopedia to include words like happy, sad, flabbergasted, upset – you know the basics. Up until this point, she thinks that she is pretty ok despite being in a devastating accident. She notices that sometimes people see her and they tend to go in the opposite direction. She is normally loud. She's never heard of the word filter, so she just says what is on her mind. She also makes jokes that aren't funny and laughs hysterically at them not understanding that sometimes the things she says may be offensive in nature. She tries to be nice to people, but no one seems to want to be around her. She isn't sure why. That's when she has learned about being self-aware, the first component of self-awareness.

Self-awareness is the master key to unlocking emotional intelligence. Once you have a deeper understanding of what self-awareness is and go about becoming self-aware, the rest of the components of emotional intelligence becomes/ easier. Being self-aware is difficult. That's why lots of people avoid being self-aware. They delude themselves into thinking they are perfect because that's easier than facing the cold hard truth about themselves. Do not be like those people. I want to commend you, number one, for picking up this book, it shows that you are open to having an honest conversation with yourself. What should a conversation with yourself about being self-aware look like? What questions would you need to ask yourself? This chapter will help you have that conversation and start on the path of self-awareness. The first section is all about knowing yourself and the second is about how to motivate yourself to become the person you want to be.

Self-awareness is important, yet difficult because it is all about examining your actions. You have to look at your past behaviors and your present behavior to understand how you can change your actions. Self-awareness is also difficult because we tend to be biased about our actions. Let's face it. We think we are the greatest thing. Do not get me wrong. It is great to have self-esteem about who we are, but it is more important to be realistic about our opportunities for improvement in order to carve out the best life possible for ourselves. Being self-aware brings on a bevy of benefits. When you are self-aware, you are able to be more empathetic and compassionate to everyone that you meet instead of just being blinded by your ignorance and personal biases. Self-aware people are able to relate to a variety of people because they are open-minded and able to adjust their emotions to someone despite their own inherent biases and prejudices. Self-aware people do have biases, but they are able to identify those biases. Self-aware people are not blindsided by their prejudices to the point where they can't understand where the feeling they may have is coming from. Self-aware people know their strengths and weaknesses and are open-minded and fair. However, they do not get this way unless they have a heart-to-heart with themselves.

The first thing you need to do before you have this conversation is to set aside a day for yourself. Make sure that you will not be interrupted because this will be one of the most difficult conversations that you will have. You can bring tissue, pen, and paper. You can have your computer nearby if necessary to keep notes digitally. You can also buy a journal if you prefer to keep notes by hand without having to deal with individual pieces of paper. You can even have an empowering music playlist because you may need it. Give permission to yourself to feel every emotion that you may experience with no judgment then go ahead and buckle your proverbial seat-belt. There are no other people who can have this conversation with you.

The first topic of discussion you want to have with yourself is figuring out what personality type you are. There are lots of personality online assessments that are free, easy, and quick to take that gives you an insight about your personality. On the piece of paper, what are your initial thoughts of who you are? Are you hot-tempered? Are you level-headed and cool or are you a mixture of both? Whatever you are, think about it and then take an assessment test. One of the most popular personality tests is the Jung and Briggs Myers typology test or the Predictive Index. However, there are other ones that you can try out if you prefer.

After taking the test, you will next want to ask yourself a series of questions:

- Who is the person that you admire the most? What is it that you admire about them?
- What character traits do you love about yourself? This does not have to be related to emotional intelligence. It can be something that makes you feel great about yourself.
- What character traits do you love about others? What are those traits that you wish you had?
- What do you consider your core values to be? Think about these values from a spiritual, emotional, mental, physical, and financial perspective.

- Who is the person you want to be? Think about the legacy you want to leave. Who will people say that you were when you leave this world?
- What do you think your purpose in life is? For some people, this consists of who you want to help and how you want to help them. They take into account what activities they like to do and activities they do not like to do when making this decision.
- How would you rate your self-esteem on a scale of 1-10, with 10 being the highest?
- How are you working on your self-esteem? What daily habits are you forming to make sure that your self-esteem is high and you will not be susceptible to bad decisions?
- Are you working on becoming that person daily?
- What are your strengths? What things are easy for you and what things do other people say you are good at?
- What are your weaknesses? In other words, what are areas that you can improve upon? Weaknesses are also known as areas or opportunities.
- What daily habits are making your weaknesses worse?
- What daily habits are improving your strengths?
- How would your closest friends and family members describe you?
- Do people, especially your friends and family, typically tell you the truth or what you want to hear? Do they think you are sensitive and tend to hedge how they tell you the truth? Or are they very blunt with you and are not afraid to hurt your feelings if you need to know the truth?
- On a scale of 1 to 10, how would you describe your communication skills? Why would you describe it that way? Give three examples.

- On a scale of 1 to 10, how do you describe your communication skills when you are angry, stressed, or arguing? Give three examples of why you feel that way.
- When do you typically analyze your successful day or successful days to see why they were successful? If you do not, come up with a time when you should start doing that.
- What do you do when you accomplish your goals or are happy? Does your celebratory behavior turn into negative habits?
- When do you typically analyze your horrible days and failures to see why it went wrong and what you can do to improve it?
- How often do you seek out constructive criticism that can help you improve? Who do you go to when you need to get constructive criticism? If you don't have anyone, who could you go to?
- What is your spiritual outlook in life? Go more into detail. What are your views about the afterlife?
- What do you feel when someone you know is successful? Are you generally happy for them or do you tend to get jealous? Think about the why behind your behavior. This will help you develop more trends.
- What do you feel when someone you know fails? Are you happy with glee? Do you feel like you are in a competition with them?

Once you go through all of these questions, a conversation you would like to have is with someone you trust. Ask them do they agree with the results of the personality test and with the answers to the above questions that you asked yourself. The trick is to ask someone who will be honest with you, yet tactful and constructive. You may be surprised that the way you value or think about yourself is not how other people look at you at all. Be sure to take what they say with a grain of salt because they have their bias as well. When you are listening to other people, do not get defensive. Be quiet. The only thing you should say to them is thank you. Combining your personality assessment results plus feedback from other people plus what your thoughts are will be able to get a clearer view if you are the person that you think you are.

The next conversation you need to have with yourself is to figure out what types of things make you upset. On your piece of paper, draw four lines to create 5 columns. At the top of the first column, write triggers. At the top of the second column, write reactions. At the top of the third column, write 'How Do I Feel?' At the top of the fourth column, write 'How Would I Like to React?' Then on the last column, write 'Steps I'm Taking.' Then brainstorm. What things push your buttons? Is it when somebody chews with their mouth open? Is it when someone pops their gum? Is it when someone tells you directions from the passenger seat? Whatever the trigger that upsets you, write it down on the left side.

Questions you can consider when thinking about your reactions:

- Do you blow up? Do you tend to yell and scream or say bad words?
- Do you just ignore what is bothering you until you blow up? Do you avoid expressing how you feel and find yourself blowing up before it's too late?
- Are you able to address the issue constructively? Are you able to be calm and solution-focused?
- How do you feel about your normal reaction?
- Do you think it is getting the job done or do you find yourself still frustrated?

- When you try to confront someone about the situation, are you doing it gracefully or are you being confrontational? Do you yell and scream or do you find that you are normally calm?

Now that you know what your trigger is and how you typically react, how would you like to react? Would you like to be more graceful? Would you like to ignore insignificant things that bother you? Once you add that, consider how you feel about these reactions. Do you think there is work you can do on your reactions? Do you feel like you are doing ok? Lastly, figure out a way to better manage your reactions by the expectations that you would. By knowing what your triggers are, you can better handle how you react to those things. This type of deep reflection is an important way for you to become more self-aware. It also helps you create a stress-management system to handle things that may stress you out. What are you going to do when you are stressed? Take the time to create that system now so you are effectively handling your stress.

If you've made it this far, great job! We have more introspecting to do, so go ahead and buckle your seatbelt. This is where things can get ugly. The nature of being self-aware is one of introspection and honesty even when it is uncomfortable. You have to take an intense look into your past in order to figure out where you're going in the future. So now we are going to take a deep look into your past.

The first thing you want to consider is what are the very best memories you have from your earliest memory to the present time? Then think about what are the very worst memories that you have from the earliest memory to the present time? Please take your time when writing these memories down and go in as much detail as possible. This is essentially a written record of who you are. Next, you need to think about the conclusions that you drew from those memories? What are the results and conclusions that you have from those memories of life? Do these conclusions help you make judgments about people or about life in general? For example, if you had a cousin that only kept tootsie rolls and threw all other lollipops out, does that affect why you only like tootsie rolls now? Do you think Tootsie Roll lollipops are horrible without ever having a Tootsie Roll lollipop yourself so you are unable to conclusively make a judgment about whether you like Tootsie Roll lollipops or not?

After you have your memories down and the conclusions you've gained from those memories, now you have to dig deeper. It is time to make two columns. Title this page 'My Beliefs.' At the top of the left column, write 'Healthy Beliefs.' At the top of the right column, write 'Limiting Beliefs.' Next review the list of conclusions from your memories and put the appropriate belief in the proper corresponding column. Which ones are healthy? Which ones are limiting you?

A limiting belief is a belief that is not necessarily true, but one that you believe based on experiences that have shaped your views. An example of a limiting belief would be that if you need to get healthy, but you see that no one in your family is healthy, you may believe that being healthy is not a big deal since no one in your family takes health seriously. Thus, you feel that being healthy is underrated and this limiting belief hinders you from seeking a healthier lifestyle. Limiting beliefs do not have to be just about negative beliefs. Sometimes limiting beliefs can be positive, but also hinder you. For example, lots of people have the limiting belief that 'The love of money is the root of all evil' which in turn causes them to have negative thoughts about money. They think if they make a lot of money, they will be evil so they do not seek out opportunities to make money which in turn would improve their life. Even though it is good advice that loving money too much can be evil, it is a limiting belief when taking it out of context and hindering one's growth.

As you examine your memories, ask yourself questions about these memories:

- Did we play a role in any of these memories? Do we need to take responsibility for any of these actions? Try to look at the situation objectively like you are a bird viewing the situation from a bird's eye point-of-view
- Can you fill any personal needs without destructive behavior? You can do everything in moderation. But are you doing anything in excess?
- Are you living for today or are you stuck in the past trying to fix any of these memories? Sometimes the past can weigh us down. It is good to see the past as a way to enlighten your future behaviors but not to the point of your past limiting your future happiness.
- Is there anything that you can improve to proactively handle any of these situations in the future? If you notice any negative trends or cycles from your memories, how can you stop them and turn those negative cycles into positive cycles?
- Do I need to step out my comfort zone? Am I stuck in my ways? Do I need to eat at new restaurants, be around different people or travel some to open myself up to new experiences? When you go to the restaurant, do you order the same thing every single time? This one should be pretty easy to answer, but another big clue if people tell you that you are stuck in your ways.

While examining the conclusions you may have about your memories, you may also realize that you have some forgiving and forgetting to do. You may need to call someone and ask them for their forgiveness. No matter how big or small, make note of the trends you see in your conclusions and be honest with yourself about how these memories are affecting you now. Be mindful that if you need to speak to someone and they are not receptive of your experience, that's ok. Say what you need to say and move on. Try your hardest to make peace with the painful memories. In the midst of this activity, you may also realize that you need to set boundaries. Boundaries are important because they help you figure out how to handle people. If you know that certain people are not good, make a boundary to not be around them. If you know that during a certain time of the month, certain things piss you off more than other things, set yourself up for success and create the necessary hedges around you. At this point, if you notice you may want to talk to a therapist to do more work on these memories, do not hesitate to find one and set an appointment.

Doing this activity may stir up lots of emotions and that's okay. If at any point you need to take a step back, feel free to do so. Then come back. The most important thing to remember is that your emotions or feelings are important. They are how you feel about a particular situation. Be kind to yourself and be non-judgmental about these feelings.

This next section is all about how to become self-motivated and become the person you want to be. Self-aware people know who they are and the person they want to become. To start on this journey of being self-motivated, we have more work to do.

The next things we need to consider are your daily activities. Please keep track of your daily activities in your journal. You can print off an online schedule and fill it in if you need to. When you're filling in your schedule, make sure that you are tracking your energy levels, sleep patterns, and what you're eating as well. Questions you can ask would be:

- What time of day are you doing your best work? Think about when you are most productive. What other factors do you notice contribute to your productivity? Is it when you have peace and quiet and your kids are not around or is it when it is loud and chaos are around you. This is specific to your personality.
- Is this time consistent or does it change? Another great trend to notice when answering this question is to think about the moon. Are you most productive when it is a full moon or at another time?
- What time of the day are you not doing your best work? Knowing when you are not productive will help you to not schedule productive activities during that time. For some people who are morning owls, any time in the night does not work them. For others, the afternoons just do not work and other people prefer to be midnight owl.
- Is this time the same or does it change?
- What activities are draining you during the day? Do you exercise or hang out with exhausting people? Think of all the things that tend to deplete your energy levels.
- What activities are giving me energy? Do you notice if you have a certain schedule that it gives you energy? Do you notice that it helps when you are around other people who do not procrastinate? Make an exhaustive list.
- Do you notice any difference in your energy levels depending on the foods you eat? Do you have more energy when you only eat certain foods? Do caffeine and sugar cause you to crash often? Does meat cause your

stomach to hurt? Does eating a heavy lunch fuel you for the rest of the day?
- Are you getting enough sleep daily? For most people, 8 hours is recommended, but other can get ways with anything from 5-7 hours. When do you notice that you are most productive?
- Are you happy most days? Or are you miserable most days? How would you say that you feel generally? Do you feel that you are living in your purpose?

The next thing you want to consider is your daily habits that are building self-awareness? Are you meditating or journaling? If not, it is something you definitely want to consider whether you are doing these activities digitally with an app or with old-school methods like a journal, pen, and paper.

An easy template to use when reflecting on your days and helps you stay focused on being the person you want to be includes five simple questions:

- Did I learn anything to do? If so, what? Try to be as detailed as possible.
- Did anything go bad today? If so, what? Try to be as detailed as possible.
- What did I do nicely for myself today? Did you say kind words to yourself for doing a job well done or anything that would boost your self-esteem?
- What went great today? What things did you do really well today?
- Is there anything I can do to make tomorrow better than today? Be specific and list a way that you can make tomorrow better than today. If the day was a phenomenal day, you can write ways you can make the next day just as good as today.

You should also consider whether you should start meditating or journaling. To begin journaling, find a journal and just freely write about everything that bothers you. By doing the work of free writing, you are able to write about anything that's bothering you. You are in charge of your destiny. The great thing about journaling is that you have a record of your emotions. You can notice patterns and trends in your behavior to see what makes you anxious, depressed, or happy.

Meditation is another form of being self-aware. To meditate, find a nice cozy place that's yours and yours alone. Set aside a few minutes of your time every day to journal or to meditate. You want to practice breathing deeply from your diaphragm and let your thoughts gently go by. You will find that your mind and your body open up and will improve. Self-awareness is hard but necessary.

For Valerie, she thinks that she is getting the hang of what it means to be self-aware. She is becoming more aware of how others are perceiving her and has begun to try and develop a way to be more culturally sensitive. She has also laid off saying all the bad words that express her displeasure and the corny insensitive jokes. She has a limited past to work with that explains how she acts the way she acts. In her case, she is learning a lot of her behaviors from the television, especially reality TV, but she has come to the conclusion that the television is not how reality works. Thankfully, her husband and children have been patient with her throughout this entire ideal and have patiently worked with her to explain why certain things are appropriate for her to say and why other things are not ideal. She has been learning rapidly but still has lots of more learning to go. As she continues to be self-aware of her actions and how she carries herself, she notices that people want to come around her a lot more than they did before. Yet, she tends to have random bouts of not knowing how to handle the intensity of emotions that she is feeling. The next chapter will focus on how to manage our emotions now that we are more tuned with them.

Chapter Highlights

- Self-awareness is all about being in tune with your emotions. A major part of becoming self-aware is uncovering feelings from the past to determine how those feelings affect in the future. Once you do that, you are able to work on your self-esteem and figure out ways to handle your emotions.
- Asking questions about who you are and analyzing your past experiences can be a long process, but they are very helpful in helping you figure out how to be self-aware. This step helps you to figure out trends that are informing your current behavior and can provide insight on how to become the person that you want to be.
- When you are self-aware, you're able to live in the moment. Practices that help you be more aware include meditation and journaling about your experiences.

Do the Work

- What are some questions that you can ask yourself when you're being honest about yourself that was not mentioned?
- Who are some people that you do not admire? How can you avoid being like them?
- What practices are you going to incorporate into your life in order to become more self-aware?
- What time will you set aside to do the work of answering

the questions about who you are and looking at your past experiences?

Here are some helpful scenarios that can help you with your self-awareness. This helps you to think through ways to be aware of your emotions and apply the concepts learned in this chapter. There is no right or wrong answer. You can take this practice to the next level by role-playing with friends.

1. You notice that every time you talk about someone to your spouse, they immediately began to act testy with you. You do not understand why since you are only complimenting the person and expressing how awesome the person is. How should you react?

    A. You should tell them to get over it. They do not have to act like a wet rug just because you give someone else a compliment. You are not in charge of their behavior.

    B. You can ask them why they act like that every time you bring up this person's name. Give them your assumptions about why they act like that in order to break the ice.

    C. You can bring the person over for dinner and then see if your spouse acts the same way in front of them. If they do, then ask them both to resolve whatever issues they may be having.

    D. You can just avoid talking about the person around your spouse and keep your thoughts to yourself. If they are acting this way, this must mean that they are comfortable and you want to treat others the way you want to be treated.

2. There is a painful memory that you cannot seem to get over. You know that this memory is affecting your current behavior and you want to find a way to deal with it effectively. The person who is the source of this memory will be in town soon. How should you handle the situation?

    A. You should write a letter and hand deliver it to the person. Then officially let the pain go once the letter is delivered. You can follow-up to see what their thoughts are about the letter.

    B. You should invite them to dinner and explain the issue you have and try to seek a resolution. If they are not receptive to what you have to say, you can move forward without gaining any closure.

    C. You should ask them to meet you at a boxing ring and fight it out. Sometimes letting your pain out physically is the best way.

    D. You shouldn't say anything. You should reach out to a therapist and get them to help you figure the problem out.

3. There is someone who is constantly talking about your weight. You already know that you can stand to lose a few pounds, but every time you see this person, they remind you in a non-constructive way and it makes you uncomfortable. What is the best way to handle this situation?

    A. The next time they say something, sock them in the mouth. They need to learn a lesson, specifically how not to be so insensitive.

B. Let them know that you do not like what they are doing. And if they keep doing it, then sock them in the face.

C. Avoid this person. If this person comes around, give them the silent treatment so you do not have to deal with them. Do not ruin your mood to be around people you do not like. The feeling is probably mutual.

D. Communicate with this person and let them know that what they are doing makes you uncomfortable and then request that they stop. If they do not, let them know that you will no longer seek to be around them.

4. You have discovered a limiting belief that you have. You are currently working on overcoming this limiting belief and have done quite well. However, you had a relapse and you are not sure if you can correct the behavior that your relapse has caused. What should you do?

    A. You should continue to work on overcoming this limiting belief. It took you a lifetime to develop this limiting belief so you shouldn't expect it to go away overnight.

    B. Mope and pout. If the damage is irreversible, just accept the damage and move forward. Having a pity party is sometimes the best, soul-cleansing solution.

    C. Try to be proactive and correct the damage that has been caused. Then continue to work on overcoming your limiting belief.

D. Do not do anything. See how the cards may fall and then go from there. Sometimes we expect the worse and the situation is not as bad as we imagine it.

5. You have taken a personality test, but you do not agree with the results. You take another one and the results seem more accurate, how should you interpret the results?

    A. You should ignore them. These things aren't true at all. There is a certain percentage that it may not be true so do not feel bad.

    B. You should take another personality test and then see what it says before you make your conclusion. Two is better than one.

    C. You should take the tests results as the truth. Sometimes we behave in ways that we are not self-aware enough to recognize as the truth.

    D. Take the results with a grain of salt and ask someone you trust if they agree with the results or not.

Chapter 4: Building Self-Management Skills

Valerie has had great days and bad days. One trend she notices is that she never knows how to act when she experiences emotions. When she's happy, she tends to leap for joy, shout, and dance. When she's sad, she normally cries hysterically until someone asks her what is wrong. Then she can explain what is going on. When she's angry, she yells, screams, and breaks things. Everyone tends to cower and run away in fear. In other words, she typically goes with her base instincts and lets the card fall as they may. However, after studying emotional intelligence, she knows there has to be another way. After doing the work in chapter 3 to figure out her current emotions, without the ability to explore her past memories (thanks amnesia!), Valerie is ready to move forward with learning how to manage her emotions.

This chapter is all about looking into the emotional intelligence toolbox and pulling out the skill of self-management. Self-management is all about how you control your emotions after you recognize what those emotions are. Self-management is crucial in knowing when exactly to use the emotions that you have. Self-management is important to know that when dealing with a sensitive person to not to break them loudly or in front of a group of people. Self-management is knowing that having an attention tantrum in the middle of a store is not the appropriate time or place to handle your complaints. When you know how to manage yourself, you have tackled an important aspect of emotional intelligence. Each component of self-management works together to help you improve yourself management skill set. Self-management consists of four different components. They are consists of your initiative, having a positive outlook, a focus on your physical health and your emotional healing, and how you are able to breathe and relax.

The first key to improving your self-management is to fine-tune your outlook in life. Do you normally have a positive or negative outlook? You need to decide that you are going to be kind to yourself. If you usually beat yourself down, today is the day that you stop it. If you are one that generally has positive self-talk, we're going to take it up another level. Right now, make a decision that you are going to be kind to yourself and you're going to work on being the person that you want to be. Repeat after me 'I am a wonderful person and I am going to be the person that I want to be.' Because you have made a commitment to yourself, you have no choice but to accomplish. If you want to take this commitment to another level, you can even write yourself a special contract. Write a mission statement on the type of person you want to be, date it, and sign your name. You can also hang it up in a special place so you can look at it and know that you have made a commitment to yourself to be a better person than what you have been.

People who are emotionally intelligent usually are go-getters. So if you're not a go-getter, how do you become one? That's easy — you put in the work. You must first try to understand what the vision is for your life. Are you comfortable and secure in yourself? If not, you may want to try a few different exercises to help you figure out where you're going in life.

The first exercise is called 'Write Your Autobiography/Obituary.' And it is just as the title states. When you go down in the history books, how do you want people to remember you? You can create this legacy by writing your autobiography or your obituary. Take a few seconds to write it down. There are many items that can be included.

- Where did you go to school? Where did you go for elementary, middle, secondary school or graduate school?
- What career did you pursue? Did you jump around in your professional life or did you stick to one profession?
- Do you feel like you were able to follow your life's passion? Did you feel like you were able to follow your life's calling?
- Who did you become? Did you receive any great accolades?
- What family did you leave behind? Were you married? Did you have any children?
- How would your enemies view you? How would your friends view you?
- How did you raise your children? Where they raised completely different than you or similarly?
- Did you have any pets?
- What do you consider your greatest legacy to be? It can be something you are famous for or something that you are not famous for.
- Would you be famous or make an impact on the people that you love?
- Where would you hold your funeral? Would it be in a church or elsewhere? What country or city would it be held in?

After you write it, take a silent moment and see if you're on track to fulfilling what you want to do. If you feel okay about the progress you've made so far, great! However, if you feel like you're unsettled and you are not accomplishing what you want to accomplish, that's also good. Now you have the opportunity to take the necessary steps to turn your life around and begin to live the life that you want to live. Being a go-getter is an important part of self-management and the only person in charge of changing your life is you. If you want to be emotionally intelligent, decide to live the life that you want to live. Do not find yourself living for someone else.

Another daily habit that will help you build self-awareness is if you are noticing and improving your self-talk. We talk to ourselves all the time. If we are saying positive things to ourselves, it makes a difference compared to when we are saying negative things. People who are highly emotionally intelligent use positive self-talk across to themselves. When the chips are down, they are speaking life to themselves. They are not using words like 'I can't,' 'I will not,' or 'I am not able to do that.' They use powerful words such as 'I will,' 'I can,' 'I am able to,' and 'I am going to.' Take a quick moment to think about your self-talk. When you speak to yourself, is it negative or positive?

Let's do a quick exercise to help you reset your self-talk if you need to work on that. It is time for your handy-dandy journal again. This time create three columns. At the top of the left column, write positive self-talk, in the middle column, write 'Negative Self-Talk,' and at the top of the right-hand column write 'Improved Self-Talk.' Next, reflect on the language you use when talking to yourself. Are you saying 'I can...,' 'I will...' or 'I will not...,' or 'I can't...'? What phrases are you repeating to yourself? Add them to the appropriate column. Then underline the action verb of those statements. Are the underlined verbs negative or positive? Now move to the right side of that line. Create a positive version or a more positive version of yourself talk. Then underline the words The Burbs twice in this section. If you are prone to negative self-talk, replace that negative talk with those double underlined words. Next, you'll want to change those negative affirmations to positive ones so that you are saying positive words to yourself.

You can take this activity up a notch by creating affirmations. Affirmations are short motivational statements that you can create. You can add this to your column of 'Improved Self-Talk.' Affirmations are mantras that you can chant or positive words that help you think and say positive things. Reflect back on your obituary. What is something that you want to do that you are currently not doing? Create a mantra and begin repeating it in order to get to where you need to get. Take out a sheet a paper or use one in your journal. Draw a line in the middle. On the left side of the paper, write the goals that you want to do. Then on the right-hand side, write a mantra that is directly related to that goal. For example, if you say I want to be a school teacher. On the right-hand side, write 'I will be a school teacher' or 'I am taking the necessary steps to be a school teacher.'

If you need a template, you can just use a positive affirmation in front of the goal and repeat that at least twice a day. The more you repeat it, the more the affirmation will lodge into your self-conscious and you will be able to make the right decisions that will help you reach your goals.

Other affirmations you can use include:

- I am worthy.
- I will succeed.
- I am able.
- I am loved.
- I am happy.
- I can do this.

- I am great and I'm working on my greatness every day.
- I am calm and at peace.
- I am self-aware.
- I am a beautiful work in progress.

To create your own affirmations, make the affirmation positive and in the present tense. You can create the affirmations to reflect your personal goals and habits.

The next exercise you want to do is a visualization activity where you visualize great things for your future. When you visualize, you want to be as specific as possible. If you want to be a teacher, make sure that you describe what type of teacher you want to be. What type of students are you going to teach? What does your classroom look like? The more detailed you are, the better your subconscious becomes rooted. As a reinforcement to this visualization exercise, you can even create a vision board. In a safe place, put up a board with cutouts and pictures that describe your goals and your needs. Look at that every day as a reminder of what you want to do. The more you feel secure in yourself and in your goals, the better your self-management of your own emotions will be because you have a grounded sense of who you are.

Another component of self-management is the health of your physical being. People think that being healthy has no bearing on your emotional intelligence, but it most definitely does. Are you as healthy as you need to be? Are you eating the way you need to be? Are you sleeping the way you need to be? If you want to be emotionally intelligent, you have to take care of your health. Oftentimes people take care of their emotional health but lack on their physical beings. How can you say you're going to be nice to people if you're cranky because you are tired? If you have a tendency to get angry, this can definitely affect your relationship management. Best believe, when you are upset, you will not be able to respond to people in the most constructive way possible. These are simple examples of how your health affects your emotional intelligence, but let's take this example further. What happens if you are overweight and you have chronic illnesses such as diabetes or asthma? You will definitely find yourself with challenges that people who are healthy will not have to run into. Not to say that people who are sick cannot be emotionally intelligent, because they can. The point I want to drive across is that physical health and physical well-being only makes your emotional intelligence stronger.

You remember the biography or obituary that you wrote earlier? How did you envision your life? Were you taking medication for the rest of your life or were you in pretty good health? Now is the time to act to your commitment to be physically healthy if you did not do that before. Now I know it is not easy if you have to switch gears in order to be physically healthy but it is necessary. Do you need to bring intermittent fasting or another type of diet that fits your lifestyle? Now is the time to do it.

The next key to self-management is overlooked just like your health, but it is nonetheless important. That is how you breathe. Breathing is often times called the life force and not without reason. Breathing is used to reduce anxiety in many people, thus a wonderful de-stressor. If you become a pro at breathing deeply and from your diaphragm, you are able to stay calm no matter what situation you find yourself in. To start practicing deeper breathing, you want to get comfortable and breathe in as deeply as you can for 10 to 15 seconds. You can repeat this exercise 2 or 3 times a day until you become used to deep breathing as second nature.

The next step to continue is to work through your painful memories. This step to becoming better at self-management is likely one that is going to be most painful. It builds on your memories from the previous chapter. This step includes continuing to heal yourself from past traumas. Anything that has happened to you in the past that is bogging you down will prevent you from being the best and most intelligent person you can become. Continue to work through those experiences. To represent your total peace, you can burn your journal once you finish. This is a representative of you moving on from childhood trauma. This will give you a burst of positive energy, a new outlook at your self-esteem, and a power to go forth in your new journey to become emotionally intelligent. If the trauma or memories of your childhood experiences are still very overwhelming for you at this point, you may want to consider seeking out help. Seeking help for an issue is not a sign of weakness — it is a very important aspect of healing. If you have insurance, you can check with your insurance provider to see if it will cover your therapy. Even if you do not have insurance, sometimes your workplace has a special hotline you can call if you contact your employer's human resources department. If you have limited resources and no insurance, you can then try to find a nonprofit to see if they offer any special form of therapy.

If you are caught up in the fact that you do not want people to know that you are going to therapy and it prevents you from seeking out help, you can look for a more private therapist. You can try online therapy which is a popular thing to do nowadays. There are even therapy apps. With a simple app, you have direct access to a therapist and you can talk to them without having anyone to see your face or know that you're going through therapy. The work that you can do with a therapist may prove more fruitful than the work that you do on your own. Yes, you can improve your mental intelligence without a therapist, but sometimes speaking to someone else that has no relation to you or understanding of your personal history can be very helpful when trying to work through your past.

In situations where you are faced with managing a difficult situation, you can try these few tips that will help you buy more time so you can cool down before having to make a difficult decision.

- There first is the trusty step of counting to 10 before you respond. Breathe deeply when you do. You can always take more than one to make sure that you feel calm before proceeding.
- The next step is to create a quick list. On one side, write your emotions and then reasons. Try to figure out why you feel a certain way. Scratch off what may be causing the issue and what may not be happening. Scratch off any reasons that aren't helping. And then what is left, you can see what you can do to improve the situation.

Valerie is exhausted from all the work that she has to do in order to manage her emotions. She feels more confined, but she has noticed that she feels better when people do not run away in fear from her or grimace when she is around. Valerie knows that she has a lot more work to do, but she feels very confident in the work that she has done so far. She will continue to work on managing her emotions and has even considered setting aside a time every day to continue to work on her self-management skills by breaking the tasks into small, manageable baby steps.

Once you get through the task of managing your emotions, the next step is to work on your social awareness.

Chapter Highlights

- Self-management is composed of four different components — physical health, emotional healing, positive initiatives and outlook on life, and relaxation and breathing exercises.
- There are a few exercises you can do to improve your self-management skills. You can make a copy of your obituary and make a commitment to be healthy. You can work on your self-talk skills, create affirmations, and perform visualization techniques.
- You can also get in the habit of practicing your breathing to help you improve yourself management skills when faced with difficult situations.

Do the Work

- Stress-management is also an important part of self-management. What ways have you come up with to handle your stress? Are you going to walk away when you are stressed? Visit your favorite spa, listen to your favorite song, or have your favorite meal? Will you exercise to take your mind off the stressful situation? Come up with three things to do when you are feeling stressed to help alleviate the stress you are feeling.

Here are some helpful scenarios that can help you with your self-management. This helps you to think through ways to manage your emotions and apply the concepts learned in this chapter. There is no right or wrong answer. You can take this practice to the next level by role-playing with friends.

1. Your co-worker begins to blame you for everything that is going wrong at work. You want to scream and shout

that it is not your fault, however, you have been working on your self-management skills. What would be a great way to handle this situation?

    A. You take a deep breath and you calmly explain to the co-worker that it is not your fault. You also constructively advise them how to communicate with you. Playing the blame game is not an effective form of communication for you.
    B. You ask your coworker to refrain from speaking negatively and contact your boss. You let your boss handle it. This situation is above your pay grade.
    C. You fight fire with fire. Being calm has not worked. Being mean is the only way that your co-worker will understand that you mean business. If that doesn't work, you can get physical if they continue to provoke you.
    D. You bring in a third party instead of trying to handle it on your own. A third party will be able to speak to the co-worker in a way that you're unable to.

2. Every time you hear this one song it reminds you of a painful memory. What can you do to try to ease the memory from that song?

    A. Try to see a therapist and see if they can help you. Ask for recommendations from friends or search for a reliable therapist on Google.
    B. Journal and meditate about the personal experience and find some closure on your own. Also, be open to the fact that some situations do not give you any type of closure.

C. You can go to the people that hurt you, explain what is going on, and then forgive them. Then forget about the situation. Past is past and let it stay there.
D. You can try not to avoid the situation and just think about it hoping but nothing can happen by not facing it.

3. Your friend wants advice on something but they are not going to like it. What is the best way to handle the situation?

   A. You can have a talk with your other friends to get them to tell this friend the truth so you do not have to do it.
   B. You can be honest and polite in a respectful tone. Then tell them what you really feel. If they could not handle it, then they should not have asked in the first place.
   C. If your friend is your friend, they will be able to handle your reaction no matter what it is.
   D. It is better to lie and keep the friendship than to tell the truth and lose the friendship. Sometimes the truth is not beneficial at all.

4. There is a person who constantly dismissed your feelings every time you try to explain how you feel. They obviously do not care and continue to do what pisses you off. You can't necessarily end the relationship, but you have to figure out the best way to handle your emotions in this situation. What should you do?

A. You can give them a big cursing. They do not care anyway. After you do so, hopefully, they will not talk to you ever again.
B. Avoid them. They are not worth wasting your time on to try and explain to them how you feel.
C. Continue trying and talk to them. Hopefully, they will see the error of their ways and be nicer to you. If not, do not change who you are because of how they are acting towards you.
D. Still be nice to them and continue to express how you feel. By treating them the way you want to be treated, you hope that you can continue to kill them with kindness.

5. You have noticed that the affirmations you have been using are not working as efficiently as they were before. However, you've noticed that you have reached a block. You do not seem to be improving as much as before, but you do not see any drastic things in your life that suggest you are progressing backward. What should you do?

    A. You should create new affirmations and see how they work.
    B. You should create new affirmations and combine them with the other affirmations you are using.
    C. You should switch up your routine and try to throw in some visualization exercises and see if that helps.
    D. You do not need to change anything. Keep going at it the same way and you will continue to notice an improvement. Sometimes you have to have a breakthrough with what you are currently doing before you move forward.

Chapter 5: Building Social Awareness Skills

Valerie has done lots of good work on her self. She has improved drastically in the first two components of emotional intelligence that require work on yourself. However, she now has to combine this work on herself and figure out how to use it when she is with other people. For Valerie, every social setting that she goes to seems to operate differently. The people wear different clothing, they speak differently and she has to act a certain way in each setting according to the instructions from her husband. She's honestly quite confused. She wants to be the same way at all time but notices that most people shift who they are depending on their setting. Her husband had to explain to her that people are not changing who they are in different settings. They are only changing their behavior and doing what is deemed most appropriate. Valerie is now ready for the next challenge of figuring out how to manage her social setting and develop the awareness that comes along with it.

Like Valerie, once you are able to be self-aware and have self-management skills, it is time to layer in building on your social awareness. Social awareness can be difficult because people are complex. They are great at hiding their emotions by lying or not knowing what they want themselves. Because they are not self-aware, they have so much baggage that they are dealing with and project that baggage onto you. However, in order to be a fully rounded emotionally intelligent person, you must know how to interact with people as well.

There's a basic need for humans to feel connected to people. Other basic needs of human beings are to love, to feel loved, and to be valued and affirmed. That is necessary and it is an important part of being socially aware. We are socially aware you are also able to be empathetic and to put yourself in someone else's shoes. Emotionally intelligent people understand that sometimes you have your days and sometimes you have bad days. The flexibility to be able to go back and forth between these understanding is most important. The first part of being a socially aware person is to realize that there is good in every human. There is a tendency to only focus on the negative in people. However, when you know that there is inherently good in people, your reactions and interactions with them are going to be much more positive.

The next component of social awareness you need to develop is knowing how to give the right social signals and how to pick up on other people's social signals. You want to be approachable and friendly. The way to do that is to use certain non-verbal clues. You want to make eye contact with people and do not be afraid to touch them. However, you also have to be aware of how people are responding to your non-verbal clues. When you touch them, make sure that they do not flinch or give you any other key that they do not like it. If you decide to touch people, a simple shoulder touch or hand touch should suffice. You want to be mindful of people's personal boundaries and respect their preferences. Not everyone likes to be touched and that's okay. Another nonverbal clue to be mindful of is your face. Some people say they have a resting angry face. When you are in a social setting and you wonder why people are not approaching, think about your face and make sure you're not scaring people off by your unintentional facial expressions.

Additionally, how you stand is another important factor of being socially aware. If you are always hunched over, it doesn't demonstrate much confidence and people will not be attracted to you. The next thing you want to be able to pick up on your social awareness is if someone is being honest or being disingenuous. It is important to rely on your guts in social settings too. If you meet someone and do not feel comfortable around them, do not ignore that feeling. Do not feel like you have to try to make friends with someone if they do not feel that way. You can also observe people by what they tell you and their actions to see if they have integrity or not or if they are playing games.

The next component of being socially aware is to notice the social environment dynamics and fit in accordingly. This is called an organizational setting and the awareness is described as organizational awareness. In any organizational setting, you have to pick up on certain clues.

- Who is in charge? Who is everyone in the room referring to? Do you see any pictures around that give the level of hierarchy so you can quickly identify the head honcho?
- Who is not in charge? Who are the people in the room being completely ignored or being talked about behind their back? Is the person aware that no one likes them?
- What are the politics at play? Is it the person who is in charge or are they following the instructions of a larger force at hand? Is the person in charge there by nepotism or by their own merit?
- What is the emotional feel of the room and power relationships? Can you see that people are happy to be working with everyone? Does the room feel like its buzzing? Or does it feel depressed or all gloom and doom?
- Are most people generally excited to be there? Do the people look like they are joyful or are they dragging their feet, scowling and looking at you through squinted eyes?

- Are there smaller cliques within the larger organization? Do you notice certain groups of people always gathering around no matter what's going on?
- Are people dressed a certain way?
- What type of language are they using?
- Is the environment relaxed or formal? When people greet you, do they act like they are concerned who you are or do they look right through you?

Again, if you do not have a good feel for this, you can also ask someone that you trust.

Lastly, emotionally intelligent people have a heart to serve. This means that they put others first and are willing to be a servant or help others out. This does not mean that you are a pushover, but it does make people want to work with you. Others will be instantly drawn to you. From there you are able to learn how to be of service and keep solid relationships. So what does socially aware in this look like in life?

To apply and continue to develop these social awareness skills, here are a few skills that can help:

- Truly listen to what people have to say. You can repeat what they say in their own words. Notice how people react to what you're saying and how you're saying it.
- Observe people. People-watching is one of the quickest ways to blend in and quickly pick up on what's going on. You will be surprised by how much you can learn just by being silent.
- Watch your tone when speaking. Try to have a neutral, calm tone while speaking. Talk slowly, yet clearly. If you are soft-spoken, work on speaking in a voice that people can hear you so you do not come off as having low self-esteem.

- Have open-ended questions that you can ask people whenever necessary so you always have something to talk about if needed. You can Google brainteaser questions and pick out a few ready to use in emergency situations.
- Make eye contact with people. Look at them directly in the eye. Smile. If they look ways, try to turn back the intensity but still do not shy away from making eye contact.
- Say hello to people with their name. If you have trouble remembering names, try to give yourself clues of their names by making associations or alliterations with their body parts.
- Be empathetic. You do not have to agree with what people say or understand why they said it, just be nice about it. In other words, always be willing to walk in another person's shoes.
- Accept positive and negative feedback just the same. Say thank you and try not to defend yourself. Even negative feedback is important. The feedback may not be true, but what they are saying is beneficial because it causes you to have a better understanding of how people perceive you.
- Take ownership of your behavior. Always be willing to be the bigger person. This takes maturity and can be quite difficult initially, but it will definitely help you to move quickly through life.
- Avoid putting yourself in situations that you do not like so you are not uncomfortable. As you get older, you realize that you do not have to do things that make you uncomfortable. Yes, you want to try new things to get out of your comfort zone. However, after being in social settings multiple times, if the vibe hasn't changed, don't feel the need to put you through future torture.

Know your strengths and weaknesses and lean on them when interacting with people so they can see the best in you. Another great way to improve your social awareness is to just have different experiences around different types of people. You can volunteer, travel, or visit a different part of town to observe more people. Just like building all the other components of your emotional intelligence, this is not going to happen overnight. Pace yourself.

Valerie feels like she is catching on how to change her behavior in different social settings while being true to herself. She has paid careful attention to the dress code and behaviors of different people in settings that she finds herself in. She is now ready to learn how to manage different relationships in her life and this will be the top of the next chapter – relationship management.

Chapter Highlights

- Social awareness is how you react to people and maneuver in a social setting. It builds on the skills of self-awareness and self-management.
- Organizational awareness is all about how you can pick out the dynamics of individuals and groups in an organizational setting. The quicker and most effective way you can do this will help you assimilate in different settings easily.
- Developing empathy and listening skills combined with having a service mindset are all great building blocks to improving your social awareness.

Do the Work

Here are some great scenarios for you to check out and role play. This helps you to think through ways to develop your social awareness skills and apply the concepts learned in this chapter. There is no right or wrong answer.

1. There is a person in the office who is picked on by your boss. You think other people are also bullying this person and it makes you uncomfortable, but you do not want to put your job in jeopardy. What should you do?

    A. You should ignore them and jump in on the bullying so you will not put your job at risk. This is what knowing the company culture and having social awareness is all about.
    B. You should tell the person to be encouraged and know that you have their back in secret. But in front of everyone else, continue to make fun of them.
    C. You need to report everyone to HR anonymously because your colleagues are not acting in a professional way.
    D. You should speak to the person in charge of your manager to let them know that what is going on. No one likes to feel left out. One only wants to come to work and not feel picked on.

2. There's someone who has told other people that they do not like you, but every time you see them, they are nice to you what should you do?

    A. You should go to the source and ask them if they like you or not. Do not shy away from the conflict.

>   You may find out that they do not like you for reasons you had no idea about.
> B. You should tell them what you heard and get to the bottom of it one-on-one. It's easier for people to be vulnerable and feel less pressure when you are in a one-on-one setting.
> C. You should just ignore them and focus on your work in a group setting. If they have a problem with you, it's their issue, not yours. However, if they continue to push you, say something so they know that you are not a pushover.
> D. Do nothing. Their behavior does not affect your paycheck.

3. You really want to be nice to someone, but you do not want to come off socially awkward. What is the best way to meet new friends?

   > A. You should hang around with people in the lunchroom and quietly listen and laugh. Then try to befriend people one-on-one.
   > B. Let people know you are looking for friends and that anyone's interested should contact you.
   > C. You should find someone who you think is nice by observing them and ask them if they would like to be your friend in a one-on-one setting.
   > D. You should look for the nicest person you can find even though they may not be compatible with you, and ask them.

4. You notice that everyone is honking their horn at someone as they pass the street. You have no idea what they are doing. What should you do?

A. You should honk your horn too. Other people are doing it.
B. You should not honk your horn. You have no idea why the people are honking the horn and you do not want to do the wrong thing.
C. You can ask someone on the side of the road why they are honking at this person. Maybe they can tell you.
D. You should just keep driving and wave at the person instead of honking. That seems nicer to you.

5. You go to an event and notice that you are severely underdressed. You feel slightly uncomfortable. How should you handle the situation?

    A. You should act normal. There is nothing wrong with not knowing the dress code. Your self-esteem should be so high that even if you were in a potato sack, you would feel comfortable.
    B. You should make a mental note so you will not be underdressed the next time. Also, try to figure out why you had the wrong perception. Maybe you are not picking up on something in the social setting that is causing you to pick up on misinformation.
    C. You should just go home. There is no need to feel uncomfortable. Besides, you can't keep ignoring people pointing and making fun of you all night.
    D. You should stay and explain to people why you are underdressed. Hopefully, they will not make fun of you.

Chapter 6: Building Relationship Management Skills

At this point, Valerie has learned how to be self-aware, manage her emotions, and identify the social settings that she finds herself in. However, at this point, she has more obstacles to climb. That is to figure out how to manage the relationships in her life. There is the relationship with her spouse, children, and extended family that she must manage, then there is the relationship with her bosses and co-workers that she must manage as well. Just when she thought that she had enough to figure out, she has to figure out how to manage relationships with her friends too. She knew that there was some work to do. Since being self-aware taught her to know to be in touch with her feelings, she knew that she would have to think about the varying relationship in some type of capacity before she was to move forward and she was absolutely right. Relationship management builds on all three components of emotional intelligence and it is the last layer to master in order to be emotionally intelligent. Relationship management starts with being self-aware of your emotions and actions and then practicing self-management. Relationship management develops your social awareness muscle so you are able to manage the relationships in your life.

Relationships vary. They can be relationships with yourself or with others including family, professionally or romantically. Despite the varying nature of relationships in our lives, one of the most important steps in relationship management is to trust in people. Just like in the social awareness chapter, by seeing the good in people, you will be nicer in your interactions with them, even if the relationship was to ever hit a rocky patch. This chapter dives into how to manage various relationships in your life. Relationship management is a three-step process of identifying the nature of the relationship, analyzing the relationship, and then managing the relationship.

Identifying and Analyzing a Relationship

The first step you want to do in managing your relationships is to identify and then analyze the relationship. To start doing this, grab a piece of paper and then make two columns. On the left column, write down the important relationships in your life. In the right column, you will want to add your analysis of the relationship that answers these questions.

- What do you expect from the relationship? – Some relationships are surface level and others are more intimate. It is important to know what your expectations of the relationship are when you are analyzing the relationship so you will know how to manage the relationship. A word of caution. Not all people see the relationship the same way as you, so in order to make some relationships work, you can adjust your expectations based on what the other person expects from the relationship as well. Whatever they think about the relationship, you have to be willing to accept their perception.

- What you are contributing to the relationship? – Take an honest look and write what you are contributing to the relationship that is helping the relationship meet or fail your expectations for it. Are you doing your part? Or are you placing the blame entirely on the other party of the relationship? Use action-based words and be truthful.

- What is the other party or parties in the relationship contributing? – Relationships go two ways. Based on your expectations of the relationship, what is the other party contributing? Look at their actions and list them. Try to be objective, fair, and give them the benefit of the doubt. Are any of their behaviors in response to something that you did?

- Is the relationship meeting your standards or is it falling short of your standards? – Now is the moment of truth. Based on all the information that you have written thus far, would you say this relationship is successful? Is it meeting your expectations or not?

- Does the relationship make you happy or not? – Sometimes your relationship can meet an expectation but you are still not happy. This metric suggests that you look at the relationship and determine if you are happy or not. If you are happy, great. If you are not happy, is it because of your expectations, something you are doing, or something that the other party is doing? Be honest with yourself. You may be surprised. Whatever the answer is, embrace it. If you find an answer you are not expecting, do not try to deny it. Accept and then plan your next moves accordingly.

- What can you do to improve the relationship? – At this time, you may realize that there is lots of room for improvement in this relationship or the relationship is not salvageable. This metric is important because it focuses on what you can do to improve a relationship. If the other party does not want to improve, you may still have to end the relationship. By focusing on what you can do, you take out the variables that you cannot control.

- Is the relationship worth keeping or not? – You've done a lot of great analyzing, but here is the most important question. Should you keep moving forward with this relationship or not? Some relationships will be unable to get rid of either for familial or professional reasons. In that case, you have to figure out the best way to handle the relationship moving forward. Other relationships you have the option of letting go. If a relationship requires you to put much more time and energy into it that it is returning to your life, you have the option to end the relationship. If the relationship is only one-sided and most of the work falls on you, you may want to consider ending the relationship. However, if you deem a relationship is worth saving or keeping, do all that YOU can do to make the relationship thrive. That way you know that you have done all that you could no matter what the outcome is.

After doing this vital work, the next step is communicating with the other parties in the relationship. If a relationship is one that you want to keep in your life, you have to communicate your thoughts about the relations with the other party to see if they are willing to put the work into the relationship or not. This conversation may highlight that the other person does not value the relationship as much as you do or you may realize that you are on the same page and you both can move forward together. Depending on the relationship, you may not have to check in at all, since the relationship is never going away and the person has no desire to improve this relationship. In this case, you can just do what you can do to manage the relationship.

Even in relationships that are thriving, it is good to check in with the other parties every now and then. Checking in every now and then helps the relationship to stay alive. This allows any grievances to be aired out to make sure that the relationship is solid and everyone is happy. Now that you have determined what you think about relationships in your life, you have to transition towards managing the relationship.

How to Practice Relationship Management

Two important skills are necessary in order to practice relationship management. The first is communication and the next skill is conflict resolution. If you can master these two skills, then managing relationships will be a breeze.

To begin communicating properly, you have to quickly develop how to read what personality type someone is and how to communicate effectively with them. There are four different communication styles. They are the boss, the sensitive, the socializer, and the analyzer communication styles.

- The Boss Communication Style – The boss communication style loves to think big picture and leave the details to the little people. They are focused on actions and results. Being sensitive and patient can be a challenge for them, but they can be sensitive if they work on it. However, they can also be loud, demanding, and disrespectful.

    Types of communicative phrases you may hear them say are: "It is my way or the highway."; "I'm right and you're wrong."; "You do not know what you are talking about. Listen to me." Their body language includes clenched fists, narrow eyes, and hard stares. They may also point their fingers. People can think of them as overbearing and mean. They can also think of them as leaders.

- How to Best Communicate

    - Expect them to be direct and blunt. Do not take it personally. This is just how they communicate to get their point across.

    - Get to the point quickly and do not get off topic. If you take the conversation off course to other topics, they may get angry. Try to get the meeting over as quickly and efficiently as possible.

    - Before you talk with them, think about questions they may ask in advance so you will be prepared to answer their questions with confidence. If you waver, you may lose their respect or interest.

    - Be firm in what you have to say and do not let them bully you. If they see you are weak, they may overlook everything you have to say and it may be difficult to gain their respect or confidence.

- What to Avoid When Communicating

    - Do not try to engage in small talk. They do not care. They may even ask you why you are asking them. Keep your tone professional and to the point.

- Do not make promises you cannot deliver on. This will drive them bonkers. Always underpromise and overdeliver.

- The Sensitive Communication Style – This communication style tends to defer to others a lot. They seem open and polite on the outside, but their body language reveals otherwise. They may stir up trouble in the background if they do not agree with what you are saying even though they are saying they agree with you on the outside.

Types of phrases you may hear include: "Whatever you would like to do."; "Can't we all just get along?"; "I think it is a good idea but if someone doesn't agree do not be surprised." Their body language may include downcast eyes, hunched, and they nod their head a lot. Other people tend to overlook them and disrespect them and the sensitive communication type may struggle with low self-esteem. However, observe and make sure that they are not being manipulative behind the scenes by sharing misinformation or gossip, crying or forming a clique to get what they really want done.

    o How to Best Communicate

    - Be prepared to answer questions about details with them. Practice being open and acknowledge what they've said throughout the conversation. This will build the trust and confidence that they have in you and they may open up more to you.

    - Be relaxed with them. Ask them what they think about things. They may not tell the truth so watch their body language. Be enthusiastic about what they have to say.

- Have clear deadlines and objectives with them so they will understand what is going on. Always ask for their input. This will help them feel relaxed and at ease.

o What to Avoid When Communicating

- Do not try to rush them into making a decision. They may feel pressured and will not say what they really think.

- Be open to the idea that they may not like what you are saying. They may agree outwardly, but not really. They may not always voice their opinion out loud. If you hear from others that they are talking about you on their back, do not take it personally.

- Try to avoid conflict. They will not respond well. If you do have to offer negative feedback, try to make it as gentle as possible.

- The Socializer Communication Style – This communication style loves to be around people. They are extroverted and like to be the life of the party. Expect them to say things like, "I'm open to getting this done in the best way possible."; "I respect your ideas."; "Let me tell you what happened at this awesome party last night." They also practice non-verbal clues like moving their hands a lot, making eye contact, and lots of laughing and smiling. Others can view them as over-the-top or shirkers.

- How to Best Communicate

    - Let your personality and sense of humor show. Ask about their personal lives. However, try not to get off topic. Hedge the questions by putting a time limit on the question. For instance, you can say, "Let's catch up for about 10 minutes before we dive into the meeting."

    - Be open and engaged when you listen to them. If they get off topic, politely try to steer the conversation back to the topic. You can laugh at their jokes and listen to their stories.

    - Listen to their ideas but be mindful that they can be overly optimistic and not always realistic. When you offer feedback, ask them to walk you through their thoughts process so you can understand better, but do not ask the question in a sarcastic way.

    - Take notes so they can look at the notes later. Pictures are also good to use when speaking with them. This helps them to pick up on information quickly since you may have wasted a lot of time entertaining them.

- o What to Avoid When Communicating

    - Do not be short or rude. This will look like you do not care about what they have to say and then they may shut down. If they don't trust you, they may not be willing to communicate with you.

    - Do not try to cut them off. Let them talk and smile along. Then bring up the topic at hand. Be gentle and strategic in the ways you bring them back to focus.

- The Analyzer Communication Style – This type of communicator likes to go into details around how everything works. They are meticulous about the details. They look at you in the eyes and say what they need to say without much embellishment. They are also neutral with their body language and appear comfortable and at ease. If they do not understand something, pay attention and see if they burrow their eyebrows or squints their eyes. Others see them as thinkers and sometimes people may get annoyed with them because of their focus on details.

    - o How to Best Communicate

        - Be organized and be on time. They will do their part to be prepared to the best of their abilities and expect you to be prepared too.

        - Provide as many pertinent details up front and give them room to work independently. Charts and graphs are good. The more proof you can provide in the beginning, the easier the conversation will flow.

- Be open to them double-checking your work. Do not take it personally, rather, value their attention to detail because it is a good character trait to have.

o What to Avoid When Communicating

- Do not use negative language when offering feedback. Try to be as positive as possible. Also, do not make personal attacks when providing feedback. Keep the feedback to the details only.

- Try to keep the conversation on track. Do not ask questions about how they feel. Frame your questions to ask them what they think about the facts.

- They may not be as open to hearing about your personal life or small talk. So try to keep the anecdotes to yourself. However, the anecdote may just be what is needed to get them to open up. Keep the anecdote about children or pets and then see if they open up or not. If they do not open up, do not push it.

- Do not belittle them or talk condescendingly to them. Let them know that you value their work or insight and they will go above and beyond for you.

As you think about different communication styles, what is your style? What is your dominant communication style? What is your secondary communication style? Knowing what communication style you are helps you to understand the communications styles better and also helps you figure out how to explain to people the best way to communicate with you.

Most people have a combination of all communication styles so it is ideal to try and pick out the main communication type someone has and then apply the communication style strategies that are closely related to their most-dominant communication style. The more you practice communicating with the various styles, you will be able to be more nuanced in the way you communicate with people.

Another major component of having successful relationship management is conflict resolution. When dealing with relationships, conflict is bound to happen. Firstly, accept that conflict will happen. Conflict is nothing to be afraid of nor is conflict good or bad. Conflict is conflict. It is a human emotion that you will run into at some point in your life so it is good to know that it is going to happen and prepare yourself for when it happens. However, to successfully manage them you need to follow a few steps.

- Wait. When conflict first happens, you can pause for a moment. If you need to take a deep breath and count to ten, do so because it could save you from saying something that you regret. When you wait for a brief moment, it gives you time to collect your thoughts. Sometimes to resolve conflict, you can wait and agree to come back to the discussion once everyone has cooler heads.

- When it is time to resolve a conflict, first try to understand the reasoning behind the conflict. Great questions to ask include:

    o How can the conflict be resolved? - What would everyone deem as an acceptable response to solving the conflict? What are the tangibles and intangibles that can cause the issues to be resolved? Are you angry at a specific action or multiple actions? Knowing this can help you get to the root of the conflict.

    o What do you want out of conflict? - Knowing what you want to get out of the conflict resolution is important because it let you advocate for yourself and for your interest. What are non-negotiable for you when trying to resolve conflict? Also, what are you willing to compromise on? If you know this, this can help save time when in the middle of conflict resolution.

    o What triggered the anger? – What event caused the issue to boil over in the first place? Was it one event or a series of events? When you are discussing the conflict, are you discussing issues that occurred after the initial trigger of conflict or are you discussing what caused the conflict in the first place?

    o What interests do we both have that will see this resolved satisfactorily? – What are the common issues that both parties have interests in that can cause resolution? Are there things that you both can compromise on so the issue can be resolved quickly?

  o Is your conflict a real issue or is your conflict an issue because you are a drama king or drama queen? – The answer to this question requires serious self-awareness. Sometimes we are being dramatic and our emotions cause us to blow things out of proportion. When trying to resolve conflict, make sure that the issue is not because you are upset. Make sure that it is because there is an actual issue at hand.

- Use neutral language. Try not to use language that uses blame language. Instead of saying words like "You did this" or "You did that", place the emphasis on how you felt as a result of the action. Take your time. Great advice is to use the 'Is it kind, it is true. Is it necessary' by Shirdi Sai Baba. If one of these is not met, do not say it. Only say words that meet all of these criteria.

- Do not offend people. Do not go low or make personal attacks. When people are talking, you can repeat what they are saying and try to use the words, 'I understand that you said...' or "I think I heard you say..." This helps the other party know that you are interested in what they are saying. This also slows down your angry response. That way the other party knows that you are listening.

- View the problem independently of the person. This is a wonderful piece of advice because it helps you remember that the other party is just a person. The behavior is what you have an issue with, not the person.

This will definitely help you not say things that you wish you did not say.

- Maintain respect. Some relationships last a lifetime so you do not want to say something that will hinder the relationship down the road. When you say something, remember that you cannot take it back. Therefore, mind what you say because it could be the source of further conflict down the road.

- Try to understand first and then try to be understood. This helps you to let the other party feel understood, builds trust and lets them know you are trying to resolve the issue.

- Talk from a place of sadness, not anger. When speaking from a place of sadness, it allows you to be more vulnerable than when you are angry. It also opens up your senses to be nicer to someone else since you are in a vulnerable state.

- In the same vein, try to be open to other people's perceptions. Some people may perceive things differently than you and that's ok. Be open to listening to their perception and take responsibility for offending others even if you did something unintentionally.

- Take responsibility quickly if you are at fault. Take responsibility quickly sometimes if you are not at fault. Sometimes taking responsibility for issues that you may have not really helped resolve the issue. This is an act of good faith and helps mend conflicts faster than if no one wants to take responsibility. This also means taking responsibility for your feelings. Instead of saying what the other party did, explain the emotion that you are feeling. This put your feelings out in the open, clears your chest, and then opens the door to a faster resolution.

- Here's a handy formula to use when expressing your feelings in the middle of resolving conflict:
    - I feel (explain the emotion. If you can draw from your varied emotional library this is a good time to do so.)
    - When you (describe the behavior that made you feel the emotion objectively)
    - Because (what was the result of the behavior)
    - I would like (make a request of what the person can do to resolve the issue in the future. The other party may be open to doing this behavior and they may not be.)

- Go directly to the source of the conflict when trying to perform conflict management efficiently. Do not go to someone else about an issue you are having with someone else. This creates more layers that may have to be resolved later on down the road. When you feel an issue, go to the person who is the cause of the issue and let them know what the issue is. Then let them know you are serious about resolving the issue. After you reach some type of resolution, let the conflict be over. Avoid gossiping about the resolution to others.

- Listen. Be empathetic. Try not to take notes while listening to the other party. It can give off the vibe that you are not listening to what they have to say.

- Avoid trying to resolve conflicts by using written modes of communication like emails, texts, or letters. This helps because meanings can be lost in translation over the written word. However, if you must write to keep records of the meaning in a business setting, keep the correspondence professional because the written communication could be accessed by superiors in the future.

- Sometimes you can let your final demands that would resolve the conflict go. If you are unwilling to compromise your requests, the conflict may never be resolved. Be willing to compromise. This does not mean you are weak, it means that you have a solution that everyone is ok with and you become the hero.

- If you have to give feedback, frame it with the 'what-what-why' technique for giving feedback. First, explain what happened that causes the issue in the first place. Give examples. Then follow up with what should have happened to make the situation better. You can end the feedback with why this is a better reaction to the said issue and how it will prevent any conflict in the future.

- If you need a break in the middle of resolving a conflict, take it. Then come back to the discussion. You're human and the other person is human. Sometimes as you discuss the source of the conflict, emotions come rolling back and you or the other party gets upset again. Take the break, take a deep breath, and come back prepared to begin resolving the issue all the way over again.

- Practice. Keep practicing. Conflict resolution is not going to be solved overnight. If at the first time you are not perfect, do not panic. You will continue to improve. You will continue to know how to communicate with others with the communication style that's most effective for them to reach resolutions for conflict.

Communication skills, conflict resolution, and conflict management skills are at the heart of relationship management. These skills with be modified according to what type of relationship that you are trying to manage.

How to Manage Different Types of Relationships

How do you handle relationship management with various components of your family? This section gives you the best practices to use when managing the varying nature of relationships in your life.

Family

You can't choose your family but you can manage your relationship with them. Most people tend to want to have a close family unit, especially with their nuclear family. But in order to do so, you have to manage the relationship. Communication is key in helping you develop the relationship you want to with your nuclear or extended family. Families have so many layers so be careful with how you manage relationships because you cannot change your family. However, when dealing with family if the relationship is toxic, you can be open to cutting off the relationships if after talking, your family members do not want to acknowledge the conflict that you have with them. Do not be disappointed if your family does not always act the way you want them to act. They are human after all. However, here are some great tips to help with managing the relationship with your family.

- Communicate regularly. Be consistent in your communication schedule. With spouses and children, a consistent communication schedule helps them to see how important they are in your life and helps create small traditions among you that build the trust and love in the relationship.

- Consider initiating a regular family meeting for members or your nuclear family. This allows all grievances to be aired out and helps to build rapport amongst the family members.

- For your extended family, try to arrange a trip or time that you can get together outside of the holidays, so you are deepening the familial bond.

Friendships

Some friendships are those that you have to speak to the other person consistently in order to keep the friendship alive. Some other friendships are such that you can pick up right where you left off. You know the nature of your relationship and can adjust accordingly. With the advent of technology, it is easier to stay in touch with friends. Just like any relationship, create a regular communication schedule. With friends, pay attention to what they may not be saying. Be interested in their lives and pick up on any body language that may give their true feelings. Other tips include:

- Evaluate your friendships intermittently to make sure that the relationship is still working for both of you.

- Sometimes friendships change and are not the same. Children, spouse, and jobs can get in between friendships. Allow the friendship to develop organically and maintain the relationship according to changes in your lives.

Romantic Relationship

Relationships can fail when people who are in the relationships stop maintaining the relationship. With a romantic relationship, you have to continue to communicate and trust one another over the length of the relationship. Non-verbal clues are very important to observe in a romantic relationship especially the longer the relationship. When you hug and kiss your partner, how do they respond? When you want to talk and spend time together, how do they respond? Direct communication is also helpful. Check in every now and then and make sure everything is on the up and up.

- Keep things spicy. Do not be afraid to try things. Of course, try only what you and your partner are both comfortable with. It doesn't have to be just sexual things. You can change your routine to add some variety to your lives.

- Set aside time for you both. If you have children together, it is important to continue to bond without them so you can maintain your spark together.

- Resolve conflicts quickly. Conflict management is extremely important in relationships because sometimes conflict can bubble, fester, and damage the relationship beyond repair. The quicker you can resolve an issue, the better.

Coworker Relationship

There is a famous saying that states "Do not be friends with your co-workers." Keep the relationship professional. That's an interesting advice because the type of relationship you have with your co-workers depends on the culture of the office.

Some workplace environments are really relaxed where co-worker relationships thrive. Other company atmospheres are cutthroat and competitive. Once you pick up on the company culture, you can decide how to move forward.

- Do not be the negative Nancy in the office. People do not like to be around negative people. Make sure that you are bringing positive energy to the workplace and not bogging it down with your drama.

- Be the co-worker others want to work with. If you are the type of co-worker that works and communicates well, others will want to be around you. This is important because if you ever move up in a company, your co-workers' opinions matter.

- Always respect people. You never know when they may be your boss. Do not let a nasty attitude come back to bite you in the butt.

Ultimately, the most important thing about relationship management, no matter what setting, is to always check in with your emotions. Being self-aware helps you have better relationships. Always check to see that you are being the best person that you can be in any relationship. If at any point, you realize that someone does not like you or you no longer want to continue in a relationship in the same capacity as before, it is your right to change your mind and adjust your behavior accordingly. Always be mindful that relationships can change and be okay with that change. As long as you are doing the best you can do in any relationship that is all that is required.

Other Tips for Managing Relationships

If you have the core skills of communication and conflict resolution, you will be able to successfully manage any type of relationship. Other great tips that you want to have when managing relationships include:

- Let other people know you are acknowledging their feelings. If they have strong feelings of anger or happiness, let them know that you understand their feelings, try to have empathy, but do not dismiss or belittle their emotions. A simple acknowledgment is great because it helps to build trust.

- If you ever get into an intense argument, focus on solutions instead of blaming people. It helps move the conversation forward. Anger is pointless. If at any point you get angry, acknowledge the anger then focus on a way to move forward.

- Be supportive. Always be supportive of people in whatever capacity possible. People never forget how you make them feel.

- Focus on yourself. Do not leave your support systems at the expense of maintaining a relationship. This is especially true in familial and romantic relationships. Do not feel the need to put all your needs aside because if at any point the relationship is lost, you will no longer know who you are.

- The most important thing to remember with relationship management is that you can never change the actions of people, but you can change how you react to them. This piece of advice will save you lots of heartbreak.

- Successful relationships take work. You will not always be compatible with people and they may not always be compatible with you. Everyone will not always like you and you may not like everyone else. That is ok. It is a part of life. Treat everyone the way you would like to be treated and the rest tends to work itself out.

In conclusion, emotional intelligence takes work but it is not impossible. For Valerie, she has learned how to develop her emotional intelligence from scratch and has learned quite a few tips along the way. For her, she noticed how much easier her life has become since she began to develop and embrace emotional intelligence. She is more in tune with herself and her feelings. She considers herself healthier in all aspects — emotionally, spiritually, and physically. She is more in tune with the feelings of others and is able to read what they are saying to her with their words and with their non-verbal clues. Her family life is thriving because she communicates how she feels. Valerie is also able to handle conflict easily without holding grudges or being bogged down in negativity. Her co-workers see how great a communicator she is and her bosses are looking forward to promoting her one day. She would not have been this way if she had not been forced to do so, but she is grateful for how emotional intelligence has improved her life exponentially.

Do not be like Valerie! Do not wait for the relationship to fail, for you to lose your health and mind, or for any other catastrophic incident to happen before you see the importance of being emotionally intelligent. You've made it to the end and the next step is in your hands.

Chapter Highlights

- Relationship management is all about how you handle the different relationships in your life. It is the last step in becoming emotionally aware.

- When you see the good as a core foundation of your relationship management skillset, you will always be able to effectively manage relationships.

- Always pay attention to people's non-verbal clues. It often states how they really feel. Practice adjusting your communication styles and conflict relationship skills to improve your relationship management.

Do the Work

Here are some great relationship scenarios for you to try out on your own. This helps you to think through ways to manage relationships and apply the concepts learned in this chapter. There is no right or wrong answer. You can take this practice to the next level by role-playing with friends.

1. Your significant other has been acting distant lately, but every time you ask them what is wrong, they say nothing is the matter. How should you proceed?

    A. You can take them for the word at it and do not push it. They'll tell you what is wrong eventually.

    B. You can dig deeper because you know that something bad is going on. They are probably cheating on you.

C. You can beg them to tell you what is wrong with them because you know something is not right.

D. You can take them at their word.

2. You were just upgraded to a manager position at your job. You have a co-worker who is having a difficult time in their personal life. Their hardships are causing you to pick up their workload and stay late at work. You want to be empathetic to their needs, but you do not want to stay late at work and do work that you are not getting paid to do. How should you react?

A. You can talk to them to see what you can do to help that does not require you doing their work. Also, make them aware that they need to do their work or take a leave of absence because it is affecting the team negatively.

B. You can talk to your boss to see if they can talk to them. That way you are not putting your friendship on the line.

C. You can be nice to your friend and co-worker so you can maintain the personal relationship outside of work. The hardship should not last that much longer.

D. You can rule with an iron fist. You are the boss and they need to learn how to handle their personal life and their professional life. You do not want other people on your team to think that you are showing favoritism.

3. Your family loves you and always wants to see that you're thriving. You casually mentioned that you received a salary raise with your new promotion. You have one family member, in particular, who asks you for money, but do not want to give them the money at all. What should you do?

   A. To test them and see if they really need the money or not, ask them why they are asking you for money. Then create a contract for them to sign before you loan them money. Include the date that they will be paying you back and the repercussions if they do not in the contract.

   B. You just ignore their calls, texts, and emails. They'll be all right. You cannot be responsible for people outside of your nuclear family.

   C. You should get them the loan. If they do not pay you back, never give him another one.

   D. Communicate honestly with them. Let them know you feel uncomfortable with giving them a loan but you still love them. Then deny giving them the loan.

4. Your friendship with your very best friend has changed ever since they got married. They do not keep in touch like before and aren't acting like they were before the marriage. How should you handle the new dynamic in your friendship?

   A. You should realize that things have changed in your friendship and give your friend time to adjust. Everything will settle and go back to normal in the friendship soon enough.

B. You need to call them and communicate how you feel. By doing this, you ensure that the relationship doesn't get out of hand.

C. Ignore your friend the same way that they are ignoring you. True friends do not treat their friends like this too.

D. You should end the friendship because they have outgrown the relationship and not being the friend that they need to be.

5. You feel a little out of whack and you are not sure who to talk to about all the feelings you have been experiencing. You discuss the changes with a friend in confidence but soon find out that this friend has told everyone your personal business. How should you respond?

    A. You should not do anything. If they are your friend, they are well within their rights to share your personal information with everyone in your friend group. All of your friends have the right to know.

    B. You should confront them directly and let them know that they should never talk to you again. The friendship is over.

    C. You should bring in all your friend and you all can talk about your issues together. But also let the friend know that you did not like their behavior.

    D. Exclude yourself even more from the group. Everyone is going to think that you are weird anyway.

Conclusion

Thank you for making it through to the end of Emotional intelligence 2.0: A Practical Guide for Beginners. Let's hope it was informative and able to provide you with all of the tools you need to achieve your ultimate goals whatever they may be.

In this book, you have learned what emotional intelligence is and the four components that make up emotional intelligence which are self-awareness, self-management, social awareness, and relationship management. Self-awareness is all about being in tune with your emotions and behaviors, while self-management is all about how you manage said emotions. Social awareness is how you can observe and pick up on the dynamics of social settings and relationship management are consists of identifying, analyzing, and managing the varying relationships in your life. Each component works together and can be improved. You can decide to tackle each component one by one so you do not feel overwhelmed when trying to improve your emotional intelligence. The journey to improving your emotional intelligence is a marathon, not a sprint. So there is no need to rush. Instead, commit to making steady baby steps.

The next step is to start to put what you have learned in this book to use. Do not delay. The longer you wait, the greater the wait to mastering emotional intelligence. Do not be surprised to see the amazing results that daily attention to improving your emotional intelligence will bring. You can re-visit any section of this book at any time in order to reference what was taught. Thank you for taking the time to read this book.

Lastly, if you enjoyed this book I ask that you please take the time to review it on Audible.com. Your honest feedback would be greatly appreciated.

Thank you.

Now, I would like to share with you a free sneak peek to another one of my books that I think you will really enjoy. The book is called "Mindfulness Meditation: A Practical Guide for Beginners" Published by Barrie Muesse Scott and Mark Davenport. It's an Introduction to Learn Meditation and Become Mindful Guided Meditation, Self Hypnosis, Subliminal Affirmations, Stress Relief & Relaxation.

Enjoy!

This book is all about using the power of your thoughts to be mindful and bring peace, purpose, and happiness to your life.

Drawing upon the rich tradition of Buddhism, mindfulness meditation is all about using your thoughts to be present in the moment and crafting the world that you want to live in. If you want to be more present in your daily life, this book is for you. If you want to heal and cope with chronic diseases, this book is for you. If you want to just sleep better or deal with your depression, then this book is definitely for you. Mindfulness meditation has been shown to have extraordinary effects on your life from your mental to physical health. This book will show you how to tap into the beautiful power of mindfulness meditation no matter if you are Buddhist or not.

The following chapters will discuss everything you need to know about embracing mindfulness meditation in your day-today life. However, an important distinction between mindfulness and meditation needs to be made before we proceed. Oftentimes, you see mindfulness and meditation used together. Other times, you may see mindfulness and meditations used interchangeably. Meditation is the more general term that refers to the practice of fine-tuning your mind through various mental exercises. Mindfulness is a form of meditation in which one focuses on being in the very moment compared to other types of meditation practices that may use chants or mantras. For the purposes of this book, it is important to note this distinction. Any meditation practice is great! However, this book will dwell on the importance of honing in on your breath with your mindfulness meditation practice.

Mindfulness Meditation: A Practical Guide For Beginners covers five chapters. In chapter 1, mindfulness meditation will be discussed thoroughly. How key concepts in mindfulness meditation relate to Buddhism, plus the benefits of mindfulness meditation, plus answers to frequently asked questions are included. The subject of chapter 2 is about how to practice mindfulness meditation. A practical guide about which positions are best and other best practices are highlighted. Chapter 3 explores more breathing and relaxation techniques that can be used to bolster your mindfulness meditation practice. The techniques in this chapter are able to help you vary your mindfulness meditation practice. Chapter 4 is dedicated to guided mindfulness meditation exercises that can help you as you begin your meditation practice. The scrips included will help you get started so you do not have to start your meditation practice from scratch. Chapter 5 is also dedicated to guided meditations, but the mindfulness meditation scripts in this chapter focus on guided meditations designed to heal various ailments.

This book about Mindfulness and Meditation will more than prepare you to begin your journey into mindfulness and meditation. There are a lot of famous people who practice mindfulness like Naomie Harris, Boris Johnson, Katy Perry, Richard Branson, and Anderson Cooper to name a few; thus, you are in great company.

There are plenty of books on this subject on the market, so thanks again for choosing this one! Every effort was made to ensure it is full of as much useful information as possible. Please enjoy!

Chapter 1: What is Mindfulness Meditation?

> "To think in terms of either pessimism or optimism oversimplifies the truth. The problem is to see reality as it is." – Thích Nhất Hạnh

How many times have we been encouraged to see the cup half full instead of half-empty? Oftentimes in western society, the push to be optimistic and to think positive is drilled into us from a young age. However, if one is beginning to become more mindful, the transition to mindfulness may feel a little jarring as it is opposite of what feels comfortable. Imagine this. Instead of focusing just on the positive aspect of life, mindfulness encourages a realistic outlook on life that embraces the good and the bad, the positive and the negative and the neutral. And this is where our book begins, starting off by learning about this effective way of living that has been used successfully for centuries – mindfulness meditation.

Buddhist monks have been using the power of mindfulness for over 2, 500 years. Mindfulness is the act of allowing your brain to rest while observing the thoughts that come and go in your mind. Mindfulness meditation is different from actively thinking and using your creative mind. When you are being mindful, you focus on an object, scene or sound that is calm and then let your thoughts gently amble by in your mind. Being mindful is powerful because if you are always caught up into being busy and always thinking about your next step, mindfulness gives you a much-needed break and makes you reflect on your pattern of thoughts and actions. It is the exact opposite of the daily living experience of most people because instead of going, mindfulness encourages you to slow down the pace.

Mindfulness allows you to know your thoughts instead of trying to change them. Instead of being judgmental and unkind to yourself if you think something negative, mindfulness has no judgment value on your thoughts. Your thoughts are just there. When you are mindful, you are taking notes of your thoughts like a note-taker. When you are in a mindful state, you just pay attention to what your thoughts are doing but giving them the freedom to do what they want. Ultimately, the goal of mindfulness is to know your mind. Once you begin to know your mind, you can begin the next step which is to train your mind.

The beautiful thing about our minds is that they are malleable, and as a result, they are trainable. Our minds are able to change based on what one is thinking. If you think the world is a horrible place, you will operate from a place of fear and your actions will show that. If you think that the world is a wonderful place, you will operate from a place of reckless optimism without being able to be realistic about certain dangers you may find yourself in. Mindfulness helps you to know your thoughts and then begin to train your thoughts to become more in tune with your long-term goals. Mindfulness slows down the grind of your busy daily pace and gives you a different vantage point about patterns in your life. These patterns can be feelings that you have in certain situations or your reactions to how other people treat you. When you are being mindful, you may notice trends and patterns that you are constantly thinking. Are you always wanting more and more? Do you feel comfortable with the way things are? Whatever patterns you notice, mindfulness can help you pinpoint what types of things are causing you mental, anguish, conflict, or joy. Then after noticing these patterns, you can begin to shape it to how you would like to be by focusing on being more gracious, compassionate, and kind with your thoughts.

When you begin your practice, do not treat your mindfulness meditation practices as an obligatory item on your daily to-do list. When you meditate, you want to be present in the moment, not treating the practice as an aggressive measuring stick to how fast you can change or using your meditation practice as a form of escapism without being willing to change your ideals. The most important thing to remember before you begin is that you are training your mind to be at peace with how things are going in the world, no matter what is happening. Once you are able to be at peace in no matter what situation you find yourself in, then you are able to start to work on yourself to change your values. Mindfulness meditation is not a sprint; it is a marathon that you continually work on until you are finally able to free yourself from unsavory emotions that are clinging to you whether they are anger, agitation, negativity, self-image issues, unfair, hasty judgments, and biased opinions and ideals.

When you are training your mind to be more mindful, affirmations are great tools to use. Affirmations are very helpful, especially when you create them yourself. The thought process behind using affirmations is to use very direct language which influences your subconscious to help you get the outcome that you want to get. When you use affirmations, you want to first figure out what outcome it is that you want. Then create a short sentence with an active word. Make sure the sentence is in the present tense. For example, if you want to feel calmer and not be so anxiety-ridden, you can create an affirmation to help. You will start with the outcome of being calmer and make that into a statement using the present tense. Thus, the affirmation would be 'I am more calm.' By using the present tense, you are affirming the future outcome. When the affirmation is created, you can say it during your meditation time and throughout the day. When you couple this practice of saying affirmations with your mindfulness meditation session, they work doubly together to help you get the outcome that you want to get. For example, you hear the term think positive all the time. It is because positive thinking can help shape your future to where you have a positive future. However, if you think negative oftentimes a reality reflects your thoughts. Our thoughts influence our subconscious which in turn can determine our reality.

Mindfulness meditation helps you shape your reality by taking the time to know your mind. Once you know your mind, you will be able to train it and ultimately free it from negative, debilitating thinking. Every step works together. Before you begin your mindfulness meditation practice, know that it is not going to be easy. It will be a journey, but if you are dedicated, you will see a difference in your life.

The History of Mindfulness Meditation

For Buddhists, nurturing mindfulness is the ultimate path to enlightenment. The point of Buddhism is to reach the highest truth by focusing on overcoming the limitations that your body has. Buddhists practice mindfulness by using four foundational truths of mindfulness. The four truths originate from a Buddhist sutta or sutra which is similar to a form of Buddhist scripture. The name of the sutta is called "The Discourse on the Establishing of Mindfulness" or the *Satipatthana sutta*. Please remember that the four establishments of mindfulness come from a very long and rich history. This book cannot possibly cover everything related to them, but hopes to serve as a general overview that can deepen your understanding of mindfulness meditation. The four truths are mindfulness of the body, mindfulness of feelings, mindfulness of consciousness and mindfulness of phenomena. Each foundation normally goes step-by-step in a flowing manner. You can go in and out of meditating upon each truth. They all work together. The first stop on the mindfulness journey is mindfulness of the body.

What is the one thing that you typically hear before beginning any form of meditation? The answer is watching your breath. Most meditation practices or guided meditations instruct you to begin by taking deep breaths in and exhaling deep breaths. Therefore, when you practice mindfulness, the first step is to think about mindfulness of your body. Initially, you'll want to start by being mindful of your breathing. Notice how deep or how shorts your breaths are when you start your meditation session. There are also different forms of body mindfulness you can focus on as well, such as mindfulness of eating or mindfulness of how you walk. These are some of the easiest mindfulness of the body to begin with, but we will focus on mindfulness of breathing since breathing is key to healing lots of ailments, physical and mental in your body.

Mindfulness of the body is just not about the positions your body is sitting in or how you breathe, eat and walk. Mindfulness of the body also involves a deeper understanding of how all your body parts work together. This includes how your leg connects to your thigh, how your ears function, or the power of body working throughout your body. Mindfulness of the body also seeks to understand some of the more unpleasant bodily functions such as urine or snot boogers or blood. The purpose of being mindful of your body is to reflect on how your body functions. You may ask, how do I try to be mindful of my body when I am meditating? An easy introductory way to do this is to imagine yourself greeting and thanking each body part for what it does. You can start at your feet and work your way up until you reach the top of your body.

The next foundation you should be concerned with when practicing mindfulness meditation is mindfulness of your feelings. A better way to explain mindfulness of your feelings is that this truth is concerned about being mindful of your neutral, painful, and pleasurable feelings. You can also reflect on how to be mindful of these feelings by using the senses of your touch, smell, hearing, seeing, taste, and your mind. In Buddhism, your mind is considered a sixth sense. It important to be mindful of these feelings because when you have painful feelings they can lead to fear and hatred. Too many neutral feelings can cause you to become disinterested and floated through life. When you are neutral about something, you are not concerned about it and as a result, it will not be important to you. Lastly, you have to be mindful of pleasurable feelings because too many pleasurable feelings can lead to lust and greed. It is important to be non-judgmental and only observe your thoughts, not acknowledge them when you meditate. The reason you do not want to acknowledge anything is that once you begin to acknowledge a thought as a neutral, painful or pleasurable feeling, you are in danger of attaching yourself to feelings that will prevent you from being enlightened. Thus, it is best to use mindfulness to observe when you are gaining feelings of neutrality, pleasure or painful so you know how to handle those feelings appropriately. When you practice mindfulness of feelings, you will still experience feelings.

Mindfulness of feelings does not mean that you do not feel. It only means that you are able to enjoy the feelings without going overboard to the point of the feelings cause you to become obsessed and overly attached to the thing that is causing the feeling, whether those feelings are good or bad. For example, if you love doughnuts and you find yourself obsessing over doughnuts, you can enjoy them so much that you want more and more doughnuts because of the pleasurable feeling that doughnuts give you. Eating too many doughnuts can cause issues your health like diabetes or chronic inflammation. All of these feelings started because of the seemingly innocent, yet pleasurable feeling of liking doughnuts. On the other side, if you are leery of a certain political leaning and it brings you immense pleasure, attaching yourself to that displeasure can quickly lead to hatred and biased feelings. However, if you are able to know your thoughts and know that this political leaning causes displeasure, you can work to be mindful that the political leaning is a trigger for you without attaching too much to that feeling to the point that it goes overboard. Likewise, if you feel neutral about a person, you can become so disinterested in them that you lose focus of the fact that they are human and worthy of respect. Hence, if they ever needed something, you would most likely overlook them or drag your feet to help them. So even feelings of neutrality can be dangerous. Once you become too attached to any type of feeling, the excess doting on the feeling prevents you from reaching enlightenment.

The next foundation of mindfulness meditation that you want to build upon is mindfulness of your consciousness. In Buddhism, there are 52 mental formations. Mental formations translated loosely are emotions and states of mind. The mental formations are normally grouped together in a specific way. The first of these formations are the previous feelings that were discussed in the mindfulness of feelings consisting of feelings of pleasure, neutrality, and displeasure. The next 51 formations are what the mindfulness of the consciousness helps you to focus on that are clustered in different groups. These include:

- Proficiency of mental properties
- Pliancy of mental properties
- Perception
- Composure of mind
- Appreciation
- Effort
- Righteousness of mind
- Worry
- Desire to do
- Amity
- Psychic life
- Error
- Perplexity
- Feeling
- Right livelihood
- Volition
- Initial application
- Attention
- Greed
- Buoyancy of mental properties
- Adaptability of mind
- Recklessness
- Right speech
- Sloth
- Discretion
- Proficiency of mind
- Modesty
- Conceit
- Right action
- Faith
- Buoyancy of mind

- Pliancy of mind
- Contact
- Deciding
- Concentration of mind
- Torpor
- Mindfulness
- Disinterestedness
- Envy
- Shamelessness
- Adaptability of mental properties
- Distraction
- Composure of mental properties
- Dullness
- Balance of mind
- Sustained application
- Pity
- Selfishness
- Reason
- Righteousness of mental properties
- Hate

This is a general overview of the mental formations, but you can study them in more detail to get a more detailed understanding. To simplify this foundation, when you are practicing mindfulness of the conscience, be observant of the different feelings that go in and out of your brain. To easily start meditating with mindfulness of the conscience, when you meditate observe any thoughts that you have. When your mind drifts from focusing on your breathing, you can call out to yourself that you are being mindful. When your mind begins to drift from not meditating, you can call out to yourself that you are not being mindful. This simple exercise is using mindful of your consciousness. It is also a great trick to use in your everyday life when you want to be more mindful.

The last foundation of mindfulness that you want to build upon is mindfulness of phenomena or mindfulness of perception. When you think of a car, you know it is an object that has four wheels and has the capacity to take you here and there. The idea that you have in your mind of a car may be realistic and based on a car that you know personally. Or the idea of a car that you may have can be based on what your perception of what a car is generally, according to your knowledge of what a car is. When you practice mindfulness of mental objects, you try to focus on the 'why' of how you perceive something. If you think of cars as positive, this positive association could be because of a childhood memory that when growing up you had a wonderful experience of your parents taking you to school every day in an old beat up, yet comfortable car. If you have a negative perception of cars, it could be because your friend was killed by a car or cars cause you to think of all the damage that they do to the ozone layer. Mindfulness of perception allows you to focus on the experiences that shape your perception of what something is so you can bypass those perceptions to get to the true meaning of what something actually is and not what you think something is.

When you practice mindfulness of perception, you want to be aware of things that can cause your perception to be tainted. These can be known as the 5 hindrances. You also want to be mindful of the 7 factors of awakening which should be what you aspire your perceptions to be based on. When all of these factors work together, it helps you eliminate suffering. The 7 factors of awakening that you want to focus on when you practice mindfulness of perception include:

- Equanimity – This factor can be described as the calm observance of things around you.

- Energy – This is the energy that powers you to lead the investigation to seek understanding about different topics in life.
- Concentration – The complete focus of the mind is what this factor seeks.
- Investigation of your perception – This factor encourages you to seek knowledge about phenomena to understand how something operates.
- Joy -Balanced pleasurable interest in something is what this factor is all about.
- Tranquility – Serenity and quietness encompass this factor.
- Mindfulness – Present moment awareness describes this factor.

The 5 hindrances to avoid are:
- Dullness – Doing your takes half-heartedly with no vim or lacking concentration.
- Lust – A craving for pleasure to fulfill all your senses.
- Ill will – Feelings of hatred directed to others.
- Restlessness and worry – This is when you are unable to calm your mind.
- Doubt – A lack of trust or conviction.

When you monitor your thoughts to see if any of the 5 hindrances appear in your train of thoughts, you want to note when and why they arose. You'll also want to note how you can prevent the hindrance from appearing again and how you can replace the hindrance with one of the 7 factors of awakening in their wake.

As you work on your mindfulness meditation, strive to attain the four foundational truths in the order of mindfulness of body, mindfulness of feelings, mindfulness of consciousness, and mindfulness of perception. This is ideal. However, you can meditate upon all of the foundations in one setting as well. So, if you focus on more than one truth at a time, that is ok as well. To truly attain enlightenment, you must find a way to master them all.

Lastly, mindfulness meditation helps you cultivate awareness of the "three characteristics of experience." According to Buddhism, if you do not understand these three characteristics, then you are bound to be caught up into an endless cycle of suffering. The three characteristics you should be aware of are the traits of impermanence, or *anitya*, dissatisfaction, or *duhkha*, and egolessness, or *anatma*. Impermanence means that all conditioned things will change. There is a constant change that you must be aware of. The next trait of dissatisfaction means that there is pain and suffering and no satisfaction in an unenlightened state. *Anatma* means that one should strive to act without an ego. These three are another aspect of Buddhist underpinnings behind the mindfulness meditation practice. These are great to keep in the back up your mind when you are doing mindfulness meditation.

Hopefully, up until this point, the case for why you practice mindfulness has been made. In case you still are not convinced, let's try to convince you one more time. So why mindfulness? There are lots of different meditation practices you can choose from, but mindfulness meditation is a great way to begin for a few different reasons.

Mindfulness is awesome because it:
- Helps you not be judgmental – One of the major components of mindfulness is to not be judgmental of yourself and others. This gentleness towards yourself

improves your overall self-esteem. It also encourages self-compassion for yourself and for others.
- Easy and fast – There is no set time to do it. It is super easy to pick up on and relatively fast to do. Your sessions can be as long as they need to be or as short as they can be. If you have a busy schedule, you can meditate for 5 minutes or however long is best for you.
- Reduces stress instantly -Because the necessity of breathing is at the core of mindfulness meditation, deep breathing immediately reduces the stress you may be feeling as soon as you begin your mindfulness meditation session.
- Improves your wisdom – Mindfulness meditation improves your wisdom because you are able to figure out what makes you tick by noting and understanding the power of your thoughts. You also are able to be wise about other people, because this system meditation improves your observation skills such that you will be able to observe others and make connections about their behavior in ways that you have not been able to before.
- No set way to do it – For some people, the fact there is no set structure may be limiting to them, but it is a positive because there is not a right or wrong way to do it.
- Relaxing and calms your nerves – Just like reducing your stress instantly, mindfulness meditation also relaxes and calms your nerves due to the power of breathing.
- Observe yourself in the moment – Mindfulness meditation allows you to be in tune with your thoughts and actions so you are able to get into the 'zone' a lot easier than before.

- Easy to pick-up – Did I mention how easy mindfulness meditation is to pick up? Once you have one session, you will be able to do more rather easily.
- Doesn't have to depend on anyone else to do it – Mindfulness meditation is great to practice on your own. So you never have to worry about if the teacher is going to show up to class or not. This meditation style is self-guided so you can set your schedule according to your convenience.

Thank you for listening, this preview is now over.

I hope you enjoyed this preview of my book Mindfulness Meditation: A Practical Guide for Beginners - An Introduction to: Guided Meditation, Self Hypnosis, Subliminal Affirmations, Stress Relief & Relaxation. Learn to Meditate and Become Mindful" by Barrie Muesse Scott and Mark Davenport. Please make sure to check out the full book on Audible.com

Cognitive Behavioral Therapy (CBT)

Reshape Your Brain to Eliminate Anxiety, Depression, and Negative Thoughts in Just 14 Days CBT Psychotherapy Proven Techniques & Exercises

Congratulations on purchasing Cognitive Behavioral Therapy - A Practical Guide to Free Yourself, and thank you for doing so!

The following chapters will discuss what the CBT is and make you learn the Most Effective CBT and DBT Techniques in order to Overcome Anxiety, Depression, Insomnia and will cover many more topics.
The information found in this book will best explore different exercises and techniques in order to successfully retrain your brain for your day to day life.

Thanks again for choosing this book! Every effort was made to ensure it is full of as much useful information as possible. Please enjoy!

Table of Contents

Chapter 1: Introduction to Cognitive Behavioral Therapy ... 116

Chapter 2: The Mind with Cognitive Behavioral Therapy ... 137

Chapter 3: Using Cognitive Behavioral Therapy in Daily Life 152

Chapter 4: Cognitive Behavioral Therapy in Action 171

Chapter 5: Dialectical Behavioral Therapy in Action 188

Chapter 6: Benefiting from CBT and DBT in Daily Life 197

Conclusion 204

Chapter 1: Introduction to Cognitive Behavioral Therapy

Many people are unaware of the term 'cognitive behavioral therapy.' Yet, most of us know some of the basic principles behind the process. But what is cognitive behavioral therapy?

Firstly, cognitive behavioral therapy is often shortened to 'CBT' for ease. This type of therapy was inspired by the cognitive theory common in the study of mental illnesses. This field, psychopathology, studies the effects of mental illness on our psyche and behavior.

The cognitive model, also known as the cognitive theory explains that emotions greatly cause or lead to our actions. This means that our spontaneous thoughts or perceptions in any given situation affect our emotions and therefore our behaviors. For instance, if we begin to think and believe *"I don't deserve happiness"*, then we can self-sabotage so that we never attain happiness.

Our perceptions of a situation and ourselves can often become dysfunctional and even distorted when we are upset or stressed. As this occurs, we can begin to think that the negative thoughts that pop into our minds, otherwise known as automatic thoughts are correct. If we are stressed about not being able to accomplish a task on time, our thoughts can turn to self-negative thoughts. Before long, we can begin to believe that these thoughts are correct and that we are a failure.

Cognitive behavioral therapy focuses on correcting these negative false thoughts and perceptions. By doing so, we are able to greatly decrease stress and begin to live a healthier and happier life. Anxiety is known to decrease, depression improves, insomnia lessens, and many other symptoms can see either improvement or completely go away.

In a nutshell, with cognitive behavioral therapy, we can learn to recognize our perceptions that have been distorted. These perceptions may be of ourselves, other people, or even the world we live in. The distorted perceptions influence our thoughts, reactions, and all of the information that we process. Therefore, the cognitive model taught by CBT aids us in mediating our responses by first correcting our thought process.

Sigmund Freud believed that behavior and mental illness largely stems from our childhood. Instead, the cognitive model teaches that these behaviors stem from our thoughts and perceptions. Some of these perceptions may have been created during childhood. For instance, if someone was bullied, they may have also been created during adulthood. Either way, our false perceptions can greatly impact our lives without us realizing.

To help us learn to overcome our false perceptions, therapists will use a process known as Socratic questioning. This questioning process helps us to evaluate ourselves, our thoughts, and situations. This will help us learn to find which thoughts are false and develop a healthier thought process. But, while therapists fully know what Socratic questioning is, most people who have not studied psychology are at a loss when they hear the term. This questioning process is actually quite simple and easy.

You may have guessed from the term 'Socratic questioning' but the term originates from the famed Greek philosopher, Socrates. When teaching his students, Socrates developed a method of questioning which would allow the students to closely evaluate a matter and then determine its validity and the truth. While Socrates most likely didn't intend for his questioning method to have such a profound impact on psychology and therapy, there is no doubt of how effective it has been.

Questions such as *"how else can I look at this," "what has led me to believe this," "why do I think this happened,"* and *"have I considered the other person's perspective."* All of these questions, along with a number of others, can help us reach a different and healthier conclusion.

By utilizing these Socratic questioning in everyday life, we can learn to overcome our negative and incorrect thoughts. We can better analyze ourselves and our insecurities. For instance, imagine you are at work and were unable to attain a deadline. Because of this, your boss became upset which led you to believe that you are bad at your job.

The first thing you should do is to ask yourself why you are feeling this way. The reason could either be because you failed to meet your deadline or because your boss became upset. After you isolate the reason why you are feeling a certain way, you need to question whether or not genuine evidence proves these thoughts. Most likely, they aren't.

After you come to the realization that you aren't bad at your job, you can question what led you to feel this way. What impacted your perspective? Once you understand what is influencing your perspective, you can come to terms with it and create a new healthier and accurate perception.

For instance, maybe the reason that your boss became upset with you wasn't because you are bad at your job, but because they themselves are stressed. They maybe are having a bad day because of work or because of other circumstances in their life.

The reason could have also been because you didn't meet your deadline. There are different possibilities for what could have caused this and isolating the reason can help. If you find the reason was that you were working on a project that you didn't have sufficient experience with, then you can take it as a learning experience. If you didn't have enough help or your boss didn't give you enough time on the deadline, then that was not your fault.

If our perceptions are valid, then a therapist can help us evaluate them in a healthy and non-destructive manner. They can help us solve any problems and learn to accept ourselves and our difficulties.

The thoughts that pop into our minds are automatic and can greatly affect how we feel. But by going through this questioning process, we are able to analyze the situation, our perspectives, and our feelings. This will allow us to overcome our own insecurities, react to situations in a healthier manner, and live happier lives.

The Connection between Our Situations and Our Thoughts

Mary had been at a loss. Lately, she was having trouble sleeping between insomnia keeping her up for hours on end, only to be woken up by nightmares. During the day, she was feeling listless. While she wanted to do more than sit around, she couldn't bring herself to put energy into anything. She had even lost interest in eating and was no longer staying in contact with friends.

Worried about Mary, after a month of prodding her older sister, Angela, had finally been able to convince her to go see a psychologist. While Mary knew on some level that there was nothing wrong with seeing a psychologist, she was also nervous. It was difficult to talk about how she was feeling and the thought of telling a stranger was scary. Not only that, but she didn't want to be stigmatized as a "crazy" person. She knew that all too often people with mental illnesses are treated poorly. But she didn't want her sister Angela to worry, so she had finally relented and agreed to go.

While going into therapy, Mary continued to feel nervous so she had Angela go in with her. She just wanted to get it done with and go back home.

The doctor noticed that while Angela was dressed nicely in a dress and her hair styled, Mary, on the other hand, had dressed in leggings and a wrinkled tunic and her hair looked like it hadn't been washed in a few days.

After talking with Mary for a little while, the doctor began to get to the root of what had been affecting her. After having a close friend and two pets all die of illness within the past year, Mary was feeling as if everyone she cared about was going to be taken away from her. She felt as though everyone she loved could die at any moment. When she couldn't get in contact with someone, she feared that they had died. Not only that, but she felt guilty. She was worried that she could have somehow done more to help her pets who had died of bacterial infections and cancer. She felt guilt over still being alive when her friend was dead.

During the appointment, she couldn't hold in the tears but her sister and the doctor were there for her all the while. By the end of the appointment, Mary wasn't better but a little of the weight had been lifted off of her shoulders after voicing her pain. She had also been diagnosed with depression due to her loss of appetite, fatigue, insomnia, loss of interest, guilt, and a general feeling of sadness. Having a name for what she was experiencing gave her hope especially because the doctor encouraged her that they could help her. Mary set up three follow up appointments.

The five-part cognitive model for Mary is as follows:

Environment/Situation: The death of a friend and pets.

Physical Reaction: loss of appetite, insomnia, fatigue.

Moods: Depressed

Behaviors/Reaction: Difficulty accomplishing tasks, avoiding friends and family.

Thoughts: *"It's my fault," "Everyone is going to die and leave me behind," "I could have done something differently," "What's even the point of living?"*

We will explore Mary's story more soon, but first, let's look at some other people who may benefit from cognitive behavioral therapy.

Lydia was recently promoted. This promotion had required her to move out of state, but she was closer to her family and childhood friends. She could not have been more excited about this change in her life and career! But within a few weeks of moving into her new apartment, someone else moved in next door. This person had a dog. Not just a dog though, this dog was large and it would run around next door banging against the floor and walls. When she passed it in the halls, then it would pull at the leash trying to smell everything, including Lydia.

The life she had dreamed of was soon becoming a nightmare. Lydia would wake up to nightmares sweating and struggling to catch her breath. She dreaded leaving her apartment for fear that she would run across either her neighbor's dog or another person's dog. She found herself staying at home whenever she could manage. One day when she had to go shopping, Lydia ended up with her heart racing, lungs struggling, extreme sweating, and jumping at the slightest sound. It was so scary. She thought she was having a heart attack. But after a long trip to the ER, the doctors found that there was nothing physically wrong with her. She was at a loss as to what to do.

And then, when she was talking to one of her childhood friends on the phone to avoid having to leave the house, they mentioned cognitive behavioral therapy. Lydia was willing to try anything. She didn't want to let this ruin her career, or much worse, her life.

After looking online for psychologists in the area, Lydia called one nearby. She questioned the doctor endlessly on cognitive behavioral therapy to be sure that they were well versed in it. Not only that, but she wanted to know if the doctor believed it could help her. The doctor assured her that they could at the very least make things a bit easier for Lydia, so she set an appointment.

At the appointment, the doctor uncovered why Lydia's anxiety suddenly got worse. Not only did she have a sudden life change and have a large active dog living next door, but the previous year she also went through a difficult divorce. Lydia never would have connected the two, but the stress of the past year had been weighing on her more than she realized. While she was proud of herself for the promotion, she was also holding herself to the unrealistic standards and stressing over appearing perfect among her peers in her profession.

All of this stress together led to Lydia developing an anxiety disorder which was manifesting largely by a fear of dogs due to childhood trauma. In order to address these issues, the doctor helped Lydia uncover her five-point cognitive model also known as the ABC model.

Environment/Situation: Large dog living next door, promotion, a recent move, recent divorce, and childhood trauma to dogs.

Physical Reaction: Cold sweats, difficulty breathing, racing heart rate, jumpy reactions.

Moods: Fearful, stressed, panic

Behaviors/Reaction: Avoiding tasks, considering moving but unable to get out of the contract for her apartment.

Thoughts: *"Something terrible will happen if I see a dog," "I'm having a heart attack," "I'm dying," or "What if I see a dog and fall to pieces?"*

As it is plain to see, the cognitive model works for both depression and anxiety, as well as other disorders or even mentally healthy people. Whereas people with depression such as Mary often experience a slowing down, people like Lydia who has anxiety often notice a speeding up.

You see this in Mary when she wants to do nothing all day, loses her appetite, and is fatigued. On the other hand, Lydia experienced a racing heart rate, increased sweating, and she was jumpy. While depressed thoughts often center on a past set of events, anxious thoughts often center on the present and future.

Before we look at how Mary and Lydia were helped by cognitive behavioral therapy, let's look at Matt's story.

Matt was not the type of person to go to therapy. Not that there is anything wrong with therapy, but he grew up in a family who never talked about their problems. He was raised to believe that "real men" don't go to therapy. But Matt had overcome these feelings and was sitting in the office of a local psychologist anyway.

Why? Well, Matt had come to his breaking point and realized that he couldn't live the way he had been for the past several years any longer. This is because Matt struggled with alcoholism and his temper. When life got too stressful, he felt saddened or pressured, or when he began to think of all the ways in which he felt like a failure, he would drink. Only when he drank would he feel free from all of his negative thoughts. He knew drinking only worsened things in the long-run, especially when he drove while under the influence, but he felt that he couldn't give it up.

This drinking would get in the way of his work. He would pull himself up in the mornings and barely feel up to showering with his pounding headache from the previous night. This left him constantly stressed that he was going to be fired. Despite his excellent performance reviews, he was always in fear that when his boss spoke to him or when the phone rang, he was going to be fired.

Just as bad as his drinking was his temper which would come out whenever someone pointed out his flaws or when he felt either slighted or inferior. While he never hit a person, his words and the volume he said at them did quite a bit of damage. This is how Matt ended up seeing the psychologist.

Because after dating the girl of his dreams for two years and living with her for a year now, she broke up with Matt. He let his anger get the best of him and ended up yelling at her and saying some things that couldn't be forgiven or forgotten. After she left, Matt drank so much that he ended up in the hospital.

Matt was raised in a family where perfection is everything. His parents grew him up on the saying, *"if you can't do it right then don't do it at all."* While they may have shown him love, he always felt as if he was a disappointment compared to his brother who was a star on the football field and a straight-A student. Even when Matt was able to perfectly hit a curveball and steal two bases in a high school baseball game, he felt as though he had failed because another kid on his team had hit more balls than him. Even if he was successful, it wasn't good enough unless he was the best.

When Matt first sat down in front of the psychologist and she asked him what he hoped to get out of their appointments, he laughed and said, *"I want you to make me perfect."* The psychologist smiled but she said, *"Why don't we try helping you learn to be happy with who you are instead?"*

Matt gulped at this but gave a slight nod.

After their first session, the doctor was able to create a cognitive model of Matt.

Environment/Situation: Lifelong pressure by both his parents and himself to attain perfection, alcoholism.

Physical Reaction: Difficulty sleeping, stomach pains.

Moods: Angry, nervous, stressed, and depressed.

Behaviors/Reaction: Attempts to uphold perfection, binge drinking, anger outburst.

Thoughts: *"I'm not good enough," "I'm going to be fired," "Something awful is going to happen," "If someone criticizes me, then they are slighting me," "Drinking will help me feel better,"* and *"I'm a failure."*

While these three cases may be different, Matt shares some similarities with both Lydia and Mary. Matt's self-deprecating viewpoint and negativity are due to depression, which Mary also has. And his constant worry paired with his need to be perfect is anxiety, which Lydia also has.

Mediating Our Reactions

When Mary first began to pull herself away from her loved ones, her sister Angela suspected it was part of the normal grieving process. Especially since Mary had lost so much in such a short time. But when it continued for month after month, Angela began to worry. When she would ask Mary about it, she would get vague answers such as "I just don't feel like doing much" and "What's the point." This didn't sound like the Mary that Angela had known her whole life.

But after speaking with the psychologist, they were able to uncover why Mary was withdrawing. Due to losing her friend and beloved pets, Mary was trying to protect herself. Since she was feeling like anyone else could die and be taken away from her, she was subconsciously retreating. This means that she wasn't even aware of the reasons she was doing it, she just knew it was too difficult to remain social.

Here's the thing, our thoughts and behaviors are not usually separated. If we think and feel one way, it will usually affect our behaviors. If we are utilizing self-control, then it may not show very much, but some people may still pick up on it.

For instance, if you are trying to act friendly to some relatives you hate being around. You could be exceedingly kind and charming, but it would probably show in small subtle ways that you were uncomfortable. Occasionally, it may leak out through your tone of voice, word choices, or body language.

This works the other way around too. If we believe we are able to accomplish something, then we are more likely to succeed. This doesn't mean that the power of belief is all powerful. We first have to put in the work to succeed.

One shining example of this is the famed Russian weightlifter, Vasily Alekseyev. Back in 1970, no professional weightlifter had ever been able to lift five-hundred pounds above their head. Despite holding the weightlifting world record, Alekseyev had never been able to attain the five-hundred-pound goal. Then when Alekseyev was preparing for an important competition, his personal trainer told him that he would be lifting a weight which he was well familiar with lifting.

Alekseyev successfully lifted the weight and only realized after the fact that his trainer had deceived him. He now holds the new world record for lifting a total of five-hundred pounds above his head.

By deceiving him, Alekseyev's trainer had been able to relieve him of the mindset that told him he couldn't attain his goal. Not only that, but once Alekseyev learned that he could attain five-hundred pounds, he went on to lift over five-hundred and sixty pounds overhead!

This is a wonderful example of how our beliefs impact our actions and chances of success. Because this is not some story of the power of belief impossibly removing a person's boundaries. Instead, Alekseyev worked long and hard for years to attain his goal. It was his hard work combined with the belief of his success that enabled him to succeed. The two working belief in hard work and belief in yourself working in tandem can help you overcome your hurdles.

Just like Alekseyev's thoughts influenced his behavior, we all have thoughts that influence us on a day to day basis. If it is a holiday and your family is gathered around a feast, there could be many possible thoughts that would influence your behavior. Some thoughts that might influence your behavior include:

- "There are only two seats left at the table. I don't want to sit next to my racist Uncle Joe, but the other seat is more difficult to get to."
- "I'm really stuffed, I shouldn't eat more. But if I wait, we might run out of my favorite pecan pie."

- *"I'm so tired of hearing my Aunt Jackie Anne talk down to me. But I don't want to cause a fight on a holiday."*
- *"It's getting late, I really should go home. But I'm having such a good conversation with my cousin Alex, I don't want to leave."*

All of these thoughts and more may only quickly pass through your mind. Yet, they can influence your behavior without your realization. Sometimes, you may be completely unaware of these automatic passing thoughts like Mary. While Mary didn't realize why she was pulling herself away from her loved ones, it was impacting her behavior. These thoughts can run through our minds so quickly that we are not fully aware of them. All the same, we can respond to the thoughts out of habit.

Previously, Mary was unable to explain why she was withdrawing from all the people and animals she cared about. Thankfully, cognitive behavioral therapy was able to help Mary recognize her thought processes and how they impacted her actions. She learned to acknowledge the thoughts she was having, even those that were just passing. Such as *"I'm going to lose everyone anyways, I don't want to get hurt again,"* *"what's the point of having pets when they are just going to die,"* and *"I won't enjoy myself if I do this activity, why bother?"*

Likewise, Lydia learned to identify the thoughts that were impacting her actions. She learned that thoughts such as *"something terrible will happen," "what if," "I'm going to fail,"* and *"I'm weak"* were all contributing to her fear. The divorce, recent move, promotion, and childhood dog trauma contributed to her anxiety. But it was her thoughts that were controlling her actions and thereby worsening the anxiety.

Matt learned that while he is responsible for his own actions such as drinking and anger, that his troubling thought process is a result from how he grew up. By identifying what these troubling thought processes are, his psychologist helped him learn to overcome them. Thoughts such as *"I'm not good enough," "I'm going to be fired," "something awful is going to happen," "If someone criticizes me, then they are slighting me," "drinking will help me feel better,"* and *"I'm a failure"* were only getting in his way. These thoughts had previously been subconscious passing thoughts that he didn't even recognize. But as he began to act on them, they developed into bad habits which he had a difficult time resisting. The first step of purging these thoughts and actions from his life was by identifying them.

Whether you have anxiety, depression, alcoholism, anger management difficulties, ADHD, control issues, or a number of other issues, the use of cognitive behavioral therapy can help. In fact, CBT can even help people who are mentally healthy and doing well in their lives. This is because the use of CBT can help make us more aware of our thoughts, preventing us from developing mentally unhealthy thought processes, and helping us to reach our goals.

One example of cognitive behavioral therapy helping in daily life is with weight loss. While we often think of weight loss in terms of what we eat in carbs, fat, and protein, there is more to it than that. This is obvious when you see that obesity is raging across America and has become a national problem. While what we eat is important, our habits and lifestyle are large factors as well. We have to learn new behaviors and habits if we hope to stick to a healthy diet and exercise routine.

Yet, learning these new behaviors isn't easy. If it were simple, then it wouldn't be the problem it is in modern society. The use of cognitive behavioral therapy has been shown to help us change the way in which we react to circumstances and our own thoughts. The techniques that teach these have many daily applications including leading us toward our goals such as weight loss.

By using CBT, you can learn to set specific goals around your eating and lifestyle such as choosing to replace sugar with stevia leaf extract. You will learn that these specific goals rather than general goals like *"I want to eat healthier"* will help you better stick to your diet and stay motivated.

Rather than beating yourself up if you don't reach a goal, you will learn to deal with it in a healthy manner. You can self-monitor to identify your challenges and barriers and change your behavior to overcome them. Many people will often stay motivated to lose weight by thinking negatively of ourselves. This can lead to feelings of defeat and negative choices. By learning to accept ourselves and overcome our barriers we can attain physical health while remaining mentally healthy.

By setting goals, an important aspect of cognitive behavioral therapy, we can better increase our chances of success. Not only because we can only attain goals if we know what those goals are, but because they will boost our confidence. If we set small goals, then after achieving them we will see that we can attain them. This helps to push back against negative thoughts such as *"I can't do this"* and *"I'm a failure."* Over time, this will boost our self-confidence and our perception of ourselves. We will be less inclined to negative trails of thought.

Adopting a healthier lifestyle, both physically and mentally, isn't easy. But with the help of cognitive behavioral therapy, you can become more confident, less anxious, and reach your goals whether they are to lose weight or simply to live happily.

An Overview of Cognitive Behavioral Therapy Principles

There are many tools you can use in CBT. They may seem simple, but if you use all of them together with a genuine effort, then you will find that you can have a powerful change within yourself. The effectiveness of cognitive behavioral therapy is used internationally to help people suffering from everything from post-traumatic stress disorder to social anxiety disorder. Following, we will explore the main principles of cognitive behavioral therapy. If you implement these into your life, then you are sure to experience benefits.

Counteract Negative Thought Patterns

If you find yourself having negative thoughts, then examine them more closely rather than allowing them to fester in your mind. Look for evidence against your negative thoughts. If you are experiencing feelings of worthlessness, you can find ways in which you have value and worth to prove the negative thoughts as false. In a notebook, write down the evidence as to why the negative thought is wrong and then you can write out a more balanced thought. Such as "I have worth because (fill in the blank)."

When people are depressed they will often hold back or dampen any positive thoughts regarding themselves or their life in general. Even if some part of them knows that they aren't worthless, they refuse to acknowledge this. By refuting the negative thoughts and replacing it with positive thoughts, a person can begin to change their entire thought process and cognition.

Journal, Mind Map, and Brainstorm

Writing a journal can be extremely productive in changing our cognition. This is because when we get the positive ideas out of our heads and put them on paper, we are more likely to believe and adopt them. If you are struggling with obstacles obstructing your progress, then you can mind map solution to those problems. To do this, in a journal write your obstacle or problem in the center of the page. Then as you consider solutions to the problem, you can write them out from the center so that it resembles a spider web. Don't worry about how plausible the solutions are at this time. Let your mind roam freely. After you have multiple solutions written out, you can analyze which ones are the best fits for you or if you need to adapt them slightly.

Analyze Your Feelings and Thoughts

If you are having a difficult time overcoming binge eating, then conduct experiments on your thoughts and analyze the results. If you are thinking negative thoughts such as *"I'll binge less if I chastise or punish myself,"* think of a more positive attitude. For example, *"I'll eat less junk food and forgive myself if I binge eat."* You can write down both thought processes and then try them both out. If you binge eat after the negative thought or the positive thought, write down the results. How much did you binge eat? Knowing this can give you objective data on what can help you overcome your obstacles.

Problem Solving

Psychologists will help addicts with cognitive behavioral therapy by creating new healthy coping mechanisms. They do this by first assessing what problems that their patients run into that lead them to drink, using drugs, self-harming, or other behaviors. They can then create strategies to deal with these problems and urges which give the patient confidence and helps them take control over their addiction.

Visualize Daily

Positive thinking greatly impacts our mental state, long-term thought process, and even our success. Every morning, one of the first things you do should be to imagine your day going well. Even if you have an overwhelming schedule, remind yourself that you can do it. Imagine successfully getting everything done well and having a happy productive day. You can do this while you lay in bed, brush your teeth, apply makeup, or whatever. But do it early in the morning as one of your first tasks.

In the evenings, visualize over your day. Remember any success or positive events. If anything didn't go well, then imagine it as if it had gone well. Forgive yourself of any mistakes and use it as a learning experience. Rather than being filled with negative thoughts of failure before bed, let yourself enjoy your success and joy.

Doing this will not only lessen insomnia, over time it can help you sleep more soundly, lessen bad dreams, and even promote a more healthy cognition overall.

Think Positive

You will often hear people who are successful either in business or life touts the benefits of positive thinking. These people never let what others may consider failure to hold them back. There are countless stories of people picking themselves up by the bootstraps and working hard. They overcome hurdle after hurdle and they get to where they want to be. Whether that goal is to be overcome addiction, become financially stable, get out of debt, or to become rich, positive thinking paired with hard work can get you there.

Sure, positive thinking on its own can't do anything. You have to put the work in. But the two working together can do amazing things. You can never succeed when you let every obstacle or failure overcome you. Rather, you need to learn to overcome the obstacles and seeming failure.

Every day, look for opportunities to change the way you think about and respond to obstacles. This can be in the little things. For instance, instead of thinking *"the weather is terrible,"* consider five positive aspects of rain. It waters the grass, helps the flowers grow, freshens the air, your roof isn't leaking, and it washes away the dirt and grime.

Set a timer on your phone so that you don't forget. At least twice a day, practice thinking of positives regarding the situation you are in. Learning to think positively about the seemingly little things in life will make it easier and more natural to think positively about the more difficult aspects.

Plan Fun Activities

Even if you are extremely busy, schedule a little time every day for a fun positive activity. This can be something simple as relaxing for ten minutes while you listen to a few favorite songs, taking a bubble bath, sketching, or reading. It doesn't have to take long, but ten simple minutes of doing a positive and enjoyable activity can do wonders for your mental health.

By taking an enjoyable break, you can recharge your mind and body and have something to look forward to. Doing this can help to interrupt negative thoughts and help you learn to relax and enjoy yourself again.

Write down a list of enjoyable, positive, and healthy activities that you can do. Some of them may only take ten minutes while others may take an hour, it is up to you. Every day, include one of these activities to help build a positive thought process in your brain and relieve stress.

Disappointment is Normal

We will all experience disappointments in life. Whether that disappointment is that the rain caused your plans to be canceled or you didn't get accepted into your college of choice, we can shape how this disappointment affects us.

Learn to forgive yourself and cut yourself a little slack. The way in which we react to both the ups and downs in our lives will shape our joy and future. If we are unable to get past what we perceive as a failure, then we will continue to live in a vicious cycle of negativity and regret.

Allow yourself to feel the disappointment, but then learn to accept it and look at it objectively. It is important to be able to distinguish which disappointments were caused by either our own actions or situations out of our control.

If it was something out of our control, then we need to let go of the negativity. If the disappointment is a result of your own actions, then you can learn to improve or change your behavior. Learn from your mistakes, forgive yourself, and then move forward.

Mary, Lydia, and Matt have learned the basics of what cognitive behavioral therapy or CBT entails. They now know that it's important to recognize their passing thoughts. Yet, they still have much to learn. Continue reading to learn how these three people are able to progress and take control of their lives.

Chapter 2: The Mind with Cognitive Behavioral Therapy

In the previous chapter, you learned an overview summary of behavioral cognitive therapy. This includes practices such as analyzing your feelings, positive thinking, spending time doing activities you enjoy, and more. But to successfully utilize CBT, you need to know more. In this chapter, we will dig deeper into the practices of CBT and how you can benefit from them.

Firstly, it's important to understand how your brain responds to cognitive behavioral therapy. There have been some amazing studies on the matter. Not only does CBT affect your mind and the way you think, but it can also even affect how your brain operates as a biological function.

A group of researchers from universities in Sweden such as Linköping University decided to get together and study cognitive behavioral therapy. They did this because we have long known that the brain is incredibly adaptable. Some studies have even shown that activities such as video games and juggling can affect the volume of your brain.

To study how CBT affects the brain, the researchers conducted a study on a group of people by having them participate in cognitive behavioral therapy through the internet. One of the most common mental illnesses was the focus of this study. This illness is social anxiety disorder and affects an estimated fifteen million people within America.

Magnetic resonance imaging, commonly referred to as MRI, was conducted on all the participants both at the beginning and end of their CBT treatment. This study is amazing because not only do we have studies proving the mental effects of CBT, but this one is even looking at the biological effects.

In the initial brain scans, it was found that people with social anxiety disorder have an altered brain volume and the activity in a portion of their brain is increased. This portion of the brain is the amygdala, which is used primarily to make decisions, process memories, and emotional responses. It's easy to imagine how these changes could affect our mental state.

It may seem as if this biological function is out of our control, but this study proves otherwise. In fact, the study found that when the participants with social anxiety disorder completed nine weeks of CBT through the internet, their brains improved. These people experienced a reduction in brain volume and a decrease in the activity of the amygdala. The patients whose anxiety improved the most also experienced the greatest decrease in brain volume and amygdala activity.

This study proves the power of cognitive behavioral therapy. It isn't simply a false sense of positive thinking that some people may assume. Rather, it creates a real change in how you perceive the world, your reactions, your mood, and yes, even your brain.

What about people like Mary who suffers from debilitating depression? I have good news. Cognitive behavioral therapy has had great success on people living with depression. The results are amazing. CBT has been shown to be twice as effective as antidepressants in preventing depressive relapses.

The study which proved this was hoping to find the effects of both antidepressants and CBT on depressed people. While the researchers hypothesized that both treatments would treat depression similarly, they were surprised by the results.

Throughout treatment with some participants on

antidepressants and others practicing cognitive behavioral therapy, the researchers would scan their brains with an MRI.

They were soon surprised to find that antidepressants and CBT impact completely different areas of the brain for people with depression. Antidepressants would reduce the activity in the emotional center of the brain known as the limbic system. Surprisingly, CBT helped to calm the area of the brain which is responsible for our reasoning, the cortex.

This means that while antidepressants reduce our emotions, CBT can actively help us to process them in a more proactive and healthy manner. This explains why CBT is much more effective in the long run and less likely to result in a depressive relapse down the road.

Post-traumatic stress disorder, often simply referred to as PTSD is a common condition which people suffer from after undergoing a traumatic event. Most people only consider veterans who went to war having PTSD. However, there are many other people who live every day with this condition. For instance, people who have undergone painful surgeries, those who have been in accidents, people who have lost someone close to them, and sexual assault victims. The symptoms of PTSD vary from person to person, but a few of the symptoms include:

- Flashbacks reliving a traumatic experience.
- Nightmares.
- Avoiding events, places, or objects that remind a person of the traumatic experience.
- Feeling tense, on edge, and easily startled.
- Experiencing angry outbursts.
- Having difficulty sleeping.

- Difficulty remembering or recalling the traumatic event.
- Guilt, blame, or other negative thoughts towards yourself.
- Loss of interest in your daily life and enjoyable activities.

There is much more, but these are some of the most common symptoms of PTSD. If you suspect you may have PTSD, please talk with a psychologist or psychiatrist and they can walk you through it. It is always recommended to get help from a trained professional who can personalize your care and treatment plan. However, this book can help alongside your doctor during your journey towards healing.

One study showing the effects of cognitive behavioral therapy was conducted with the participation of one-hundred children who were suffering from PTSD after being sexually assaulted. They had the children go into therapy, some with their mothers present and others with solely the therapist. Their condition was checked at regular intervals to see how the children were healing from the trauma.

The children completed tests both before, during, and after the treatment periods. After the original cognitive behavioral therapy, the children's tests scores improved significantly. These continued to improve over the following two years. This suggests that CBT is a successful treatment option for long-term improvement and care.

But in order to receive these benefits, it is important to understand in-depth how to utilize cognitive behavioral therapy. This therapy is a powerful tool and if you understand its basis and how to follow it through, you can experience amazing benefits.

While cognitive behavioral therapy involves some positive

thinking, there is more to it than that. In fact, if you tell a person who is depressed, anxious, stressed, or suffering from trauma simply "just think positively," it will only cause them further stress. This is because positive thoughts alone are not enough to cause lasting change. When a person tries this and it doesn't work, they are likely to feel frustrated. This down-spiral further increases negative thoughts. Instead, it is important to practice using your mind as a tool over your mood. This will help you to consider all the information you have access to from various angles. If you are able to consider a situation (whether negative or positive) from all sides, then you can find a new understanding and solutions to your problems.

A good example of this is Lydia. If she simply told herself "I won't have anxiety when I see the neighbor's dog. I'm perfectly fine," she would be unrealistic and wouldn't be prepared for the anxiety she is likely to face once she sees the dog. Once she begins to feel anxiety upon seeing the dog, Lydia may end up feeling like a failure. Even a small amount of anxiety will make her feel as if there is no point to positive thinking.

Instead, Lydia will do better if she studies the situation from all sides and then decides on a solution for how to react if she becomes anxious. She can then think positively trusting in herself and her plan to help get her through coming across dogs. This is more successful because if we only allow false positive thoughts, then we will be unprepared for difficult situations.

Identifying your thoughts and then analyzing, testing, considering alternatives, and using your mind over your mood are important aspects of CBT. Although it is equally important to make behavioral changes along with these, it is important to keep in mind that cognitive behavioral therapy is consists of many components. Just like the inner pieces of a clock, CBT is only successful when all of the parts are working together.

Work on identifying your thoughts and analyzing them, thinking more positively, coming up with plans to reduce anxiety, and more. But also makes changes in your life. These changes will vary from person to person.

Rather than avoiding all dogs, Lydia could try acclimating to friendly small dogs until she feels comfortable. This will help her overcome her fear overtime and learn how to better manage her anxiety.

Mary needs to make a point of communicating with friends and spending time doing enjoyable activities. Her depression may make her feel like doing nothing but lying in bed and staring at the ceiling. But in order to improve the depression, she needs to get back out into life.

With Matt's alcoholism, he shouldn't keep alcohol around the house or go to bars. Instead, he needs to make a goal of becoming sober and attend regular meetings for alcoholics.

Likewise, if someone is being abused, they shouldn't simply "think happy thoughts" and become more submissive to their oppressor. Instead, their focus should be on finding a safe way to escape the abusive situation.

Now that you understand that this process is not solely about a false and short lasting positive thinking, it is time to address our negative thought processes. These thoughts control our actions in many ways. Maybe you were too scared to follow the career of your dreams because you might fail. Perhaps you become so overwhelmed that you procrastinate constantly. Or maybe you begin binge eating because you ate a single cookie and feel like a failure so what even is the point? All of these negative thoughts and more are damaging. Over time, they not only prevent us from attaining our goals and the life we desire, but they also will increasingly affect our mental health.

This is because of our negative thoughts and circumstances will accumulate. This shows in Lydia's story, where her trauma of dogs didn't surface until after she had been through a stressful divorce, move, and promotion. After all of the negative thoughts and emotions of the past year accumulated, she was unable to handle the anxiety and it manifested by bringing back her childhood trauma.

These thoughts can also combine in ways that make us think more negatively of ourselves such as in Matt's case, or as if there is no point in doing anything, like with Mary.

It is important to recognize all of your negative thoughts and learn to analyze and test them and then overcome them. But to do that, first, you need to know how to recognize them. There are ten main types of negative thoughts. Many people will experience most, if not all of these from time to time. But people often fall into centering on one or two types of negative thoughts.

These include:

1. Focusing on the Negative: *"Everything always goes wrong, life is just one disappointment after another."*

2. Negative Labeling of Yourself: *"I'm a terrible person and a failure. If people knew who I really was, they would leave me."*

3. Perfectionism: *"I have to do everything perfectly, otherwise I am a failure. I can't let anyone see anything of mine unless it's perfect."*

4. Constant Approval Needed: *"I have to make everyone like me. That's the only way I can be happy."*

5. Worst Case Scenario: *"Everything is going to be a

disaster. It can't go well. I'm doomed."

6. Ignoring the Present: *"I'll take care of myself later. For now, I have a list of things to accomplish."*

7. Other People Should Do What I Think: *"My friend shouldn't be posting so many photos of her boyfriend on social media. My adult daughter shouldn't be pursuing that career. That stranger shouldn't be wearing that, it's unflattering."*

8. Mind Reader: *"Other people must hate me, otherwise they wouldn't behave that way."*

9. Living in the Past: *"I'm miserable. I'm going to lay here and think about what happened to make me feel this way."*

10. Glass Half Empty: *"I don't trust people who are happy. If anything good ever happens in my life, then it is all going to be destroyed."*

The thoughts will vary from person to person depending on their situation. But most people will fit into at least one or two of these categories. After we figure out how we think, we can begin to counteract it. To do this, we start by finding the deceptions within those thought patterns.

Keep a little notbook with you or simply use a smartphone and keep track of your negative thoughts. You want a list that resembles sections titled:

- Situation
- Mood
- Automatic Thoughts or Images
- Evidence that Supports my Thoughts
- Evidence that Disproves my Thoughts

- Alternative Healthy Thoughts
- New Mood

When creating this list, you should use the four W's to help you. This means always fill out who, what, when, and where. You want to be specific, because if you simply state that it was happening "all day," then you are unable to target the cause behind the feelings. But if you know that you felt this way at 8:30 am when you were on your way to work, this narrows things down greatly.

Under the mood column, write any and all of the moods you were feeling at the time. You may have been feeling overwhelmed, depressed, anxious, sad, hurt, nervous, angry, or other emotions. When listing these, it is beneficial to rate them on a score of zero to one-hundred. These allow people who experience panic or anxiety attacks to log the severity.

Under the automatic thoughts or images, write any of the thoughts that were going through your head at the time. Taking the example from a moment ago, imagine that the thoughts running through your mind on the way to work that triggered this were *"I'm going to be late," "They'll fire me and then I won't have a job,"* and *"I'm worthless"*. If these thoughts were running through your head, you would write them down in this column and then analyze them in the following columns.

Next, tie together the columns for automatic thoughts and mood together on a rating of zero to one-hundred. For each thought, rate how it made you feel. Did the thought of being late makes you twenty percent anxious? The thought of being fired and without a job eighty percent scared? The thought of being worthless ninety percent depressed? By ranking the emotions tied to each of these thoughts, you can learn to better recognize damaging thoughts and proceed to overcome them.

The following step is one of the most important in this method and that is analyzing the evidence on whether or not your feelings are true or false. This can help us learn to identify what is a fact rather than our interpretation of a situation. There are many questions you can ask yourself to analyze these thoughts, but in the example we have been exploring, you might ask "Do I know I won't make it to work on time," "Are they likely to fire someone for being late once," "am I blaming myself for something out of my control," "When I'm not feeling this way, what do I think of this situation," "Are there any positives about myself that I am ignoring", and "If my best friend knew how I was feeling, what would they say?"

After analyzing the thought, you can fill in the alternative healthy thought section. Here, if you found that your thoughts weren't true, then you could fill in a more accurate thought. This might be "I haven't been late this year and my boss loves me, they are unlikely to fire me. I know I'm not worthless, every person has value and I have learned to be kind and compassionate. I am a valuable person"

If your thoughts were partially true, take the new information to write a more balanced view. For instance "my boss won't be happy, but I doubt I will be without a job. I may have slept through my alarm this morning, but that doesn't negate my intrinsic worth as a human being. I can take steps to wake up on time in the future."

After you analyze your thoughts and create new healthier and more balanced thoughts, you can rate how the new thoughts make you feel on a level of zero to one-hundred like you did with the original thought.

While this forum will change moment by moment for any given person, depending on the situations they are going through, let's look at what it might look like if Mary and Matt filled out this forum.

Mary:

- **Situation:**
  Didn't answer the phone when a friend called at noon.

- **Mood:**
  Depressed ninety percent, anxious thirty percent, worthlessness fifty percent.

- **Automatic Thoughts or Images:**
  "I can't be close to people. If I am, they'll die and I'll lose them," "I'm bad luck to have around," "Why am I even alive?"

- **Evidence that Supports my Thoughts:**
  My loved ones keep dying.

- **Evidence that Disproves my Thoughts:**
  Death is a part of life.
  My friends and pets were ill.
  I cared for them as best as I could do while they were alive.
  Their deaths were out of my hands.
  People aren't bad or good luck.
  Everyone is alive for a purpose.
  My friends care about me and want me around.

- **Alternative Healthy Thoughts:**
  "I'm sad that they died, but it wasn't my fault and I can't blame myself. My friends care about me and if I wasn't around, they would be sad."

- **New Mood:**
  Depressed forty percent, sad twenty percent, hopeful twenty percent.

As you can see, Mary may not feel all better, but she is working through her emotions. Her thoughts and mood are more stable now and she is reminded of why she is alive.

Now, let's look at Matt:

- **Situation:**
  His ex-girlfriend came by for a box of her stuff at 6 pm.

- **Mood:**
  Angry eighty percent, sad fifty percent.

- **Automatic Thoughts or Images:**
  "Why did she have to come by tonight when I was already having a bad day? She should have known it was too soon to see each other, now I miss her even more. This is her fault. If she had only forgiven me. I want a drink."

- **Evidence that Supports my Thoughts:**
  I apologized, she could have forgiven me.

- **Evidence that Disproves my Thoughts:**
  She needed her stuff and had a right to come get it. Even after the breakup, she was being kind and asked how I was doing.
  The breakup isn't her fault. She stuck with me for two years despite my drinking and anger.
  She doesn't have to forgive me and even if she has, that doesn't mean she is required to stay with me.

- **Alternative Healthy Thoughts:**
  "I'm sad that we broke up, but I hope she lives a happy life. Now that I am single, I can focus on bettering my own life, becoming sober, and controlling my temper. This is better for both of us in the long-run. A drink won't help me and I want to stay sober."

- **New Mood:**
  Sad fifteen percent, encouraged twenty percent, motivated fifty percent.

While Matt began the process as angry, as he worked through his feelings, whether they were true or false and developed a healthier alternative thought, he was able to work through his anger. This helped him to accept the breakup at the moment and encouraged him to stay sober. He may struggle with his anger and the breakup from time to time in the future, but if he continues to get through it in this healthy manner, then he can improve his life, learn to control his anger, and resist alcohol. Over time, the breakup will begin to hurt less.

It is important to retain awareness of your own mental state. To do this, try to fill out this forum regularly, especially whenever you notice your mood is low or your thoughts are destructive. But sometimes it can be hard to start because we are greatly lacking an awareness of our thoughts. This can be especially true when we have been living with a condition such as depression or anxiety for a long time. We become so accustomed to it that it turns into background noise. We need to learn to listen into this background noise so that we can tune it into a beautiful melody rather than a high-pitched static. Asking different questions based on our moods can help.

Generalized questions are a good place to start because you can ask them of yourself, no matter what your mood is. You may find it difficult to place a finger on exactly what you had been thinking of prior to a mood shift, but with some time, you will become an expert at realizing and recalling what is impacting your mood. After practice, many people will be able to place their finger on what upset them simply by answering these two questions:

- What was the last thing going through my mind before I noticed my mood shift?
- What memories or images was I experiencing?

The second question is regarding images and memories

because many people find that their strongest mood shifts aren't a response to a specific thought. Rather, it was a response to a memory or image they thought of. For instance, for a split second, someone could remember a still image of a loved one in the hospital. If you have a lot going on in your life, it is easy to get distracted and not remember what triggered it, but the negative emotions remain. This is why it's important to learn to target and analyze what is affecting you.

After answering the generalized questions, you can answer some more specific mood-related questions.

When people are anxious, they often consider worst-case scenarios of what could happen in the near or distant future. We overestimate what could go wrong while simultaneously underestimating ourselves. When you find yourself anxious, scared, or nervous, then ask yourself *"what am I afraid might happen?"* and *"what is the worst that could happen?"*

If you find yourself depressed, it is easy to be self-critical or even hate yourself completely. In this case, it's easy to not just be critical about ourselves, but life in general as well. Therefore, if you are feeling depressed, sad, discouraged, or disappointed, I want you to ask yourself three questions. *"What does this mean about me?"*, *"What does this mean about my future?"*, and *"What does this mean about life?"*

People often feel guilt or shame in conjunction with their actions even if they didn't do anything wrong. For instance, people can have survivor's guilt if someone close to them died yet they survived. There was nothing wrong with them surviving and they couldn't have saved the other person, yet they feel guilty. Though these feelings can, of course, have validity as well. If you got into a fight with your sibling, you could feel guilty for something you said. If you find yourself feeling this way, ask yourself *"Did I hurt someone, break a law/rule, not have done something I should have, or otherwise gone against my moral code?", "What does this mean about how others feel about me?", "What do I think or believe about myself?",* and *"What would other people think if they knew?"*

We can often feel angry, irritated, or resentful if we have felt as if someone has harmed us in some way. Even if the person wasn't unjust or mistreating us, we can often feel antsy from anger. It is important to distinguish whether or not this anger is justified. There is righteous anger. For instance, we can be angry when we learn of a child being abused. Non-righteous anger would be us getting angry that the cheeseburger that we ordered had pickles when we asked for no pickles. Sure, the person who made the cheeseburger made a mistake, but it is not something to get upset about if they are willing to fix it for us. If you are having anger related feelings, ask yourself *"What does this mean about other people?"* and *"What does this mean about how other people feel about me?"*

By asking yourself these questions, you will learn to recognize your emotions and the thoughts, memories, and images that trigger them. While what other people do and say can impact our emotions, remember that it is ultimately how we respond to those people that impact our long-term emotional state.

Occasionally, you may want to try looking over some of the other questions that aren't in your emotional category. For instance, if you are feeling anxious, you still may benefit by asking yourself the depression questions. Over time, you may even develop some of your own questions which you find is helping you to identify why you are feeling or reacting in specific ways.

Chapter 3: Using Cognitive Behavioral Therapy in Daily Life

As children are growing up they are taught to think about what they might want to become when they grow up. Later on, they create career goals, learn about those careers, and are urged to choose a college major that applies to their field of choice. When applying to college, these now young adults spend lengths of time analyzing all of the benefits of their chosen college, but also of other colleges. Just in case, they are urged to send out letters to multiple colleges in case they don't get into their college of choice.

All of this is done because having goals is important. Without goals, we have no idea where we are going to end up or get there along the way. It may be fine to not have a goal when you are going on a stroll. But when it comes to your life and how you spend your years, you want to put a thought into it. If someone decides to work a retail job and spend their free time painting and growing plants, that is fine.

Someone else may have a goal of becoming a leading neurosurgeon. Neither goal is superior to the other. Simply, having a goal will help to motivate you and help you take steps to achieve your dream.

You picked up this book for a reason, what was it? Maybe a friend recommended it to you and you decided to give it a chance. But what within your heart made you decide to give it a chance? There is something in all of our lives that we feel dissatisfied with. Is your relationship with your parents strained? Do you have insomnia? Are you depressed? Do you find yourself relying on alcohol or drugs? Do you have a difficult time controlling your temper? If you can isolate the problems that led you to pick up this book, then you can more easily create meaningful goals.

To find your goals, try picking up a piece of paper and pen. Begin to write down goals as specific as you can. Goals such as "have less anxiety," "sleep better," "overcome my depression," and "create deeper relationships" are good.

Although to create great goals, you will want to be more specific. As you can see, the goals above can work for most anyone, so try to tailor your goals for you. This could mean you write "be around dogs without having anxiety attacks," "overcome the depression so that I can feel happy daily again," "reduce insomnia so that I can get seven hours of sleep every night," or "deepen my relationship with my parents so that I'm not stressed to be around them and we can easily chat."

With these more specific goals, you can have a better idea of how to attain them, as well as having the ability to track your progress.

After you write down your goals, write down the advantages of attaining them and the disadvantages of failing to attain them. This will help to motivate you further. It can also help you narrow down further goals that you might want to add to your goal list.

It is important to write this down, not just keep it as a mental list. There may not seem to be much of a difference, but the impacting of writing down your goal is huge. In fact, a professor at the Dominican University in California, Dr. Gail Matthews, recently studied this subject.

Dr. Matthews conducted this study on over two-hundred and sixty people. These people came from all around the world, different walks of lives, and a variety of careers. The results were astounding. While Dr. Matthews hypothesized that those who wrote down their goals would reach success at a higher rate, they did so at a remarkably higher level. The act of writing goals down is so significant, that people are forty-two percent more likely to achieve a goal if they write it down on a regular basis.

This statistic increases even further for people who share their goals with friends or family. Having someone who believes in you and your ability to succeed is powerful.

When creating goals, try to keep four aspects in mind. These will help your goals to be more powerful, helping you to measure your progress, stay encouraged, and eventually attain what you dream of.

Reflect on Your Life and Situation

We can only know where we want to be if we first know where we are currently at. Just like an ostrich is unable to see its surroundings and destination when it buries its head in the sand, we are unable to see where we want to end up if we are in denial of our life and mental health. Take some time with a pen and paper and honestly consider every aspect of your life. After considering different aspects, ask yourself if you are okay with that. If you aren't okay with portions of your life, then write them down.

You may need to take a week in order to honestly evaluate yourself and your goals and that is alright. It takes time to consider where we are at truthfully. See this as an opportunity for growth and improvement and get excited!

Know Your Dreams

In our modern society, most of us are constantly rushing. Whether we have jobs, family, sporting events, classes, kids, hobbies, or social lives to keep us busy, most of us find we have too few hours in the day. But humans also have an amazing ability to dream and create goals.

Honestly consider what these dreams and goals are. You may need to find some time to slow down in order to accomplish this. After all, you can't very well consider your dreams if you are being overwhelmed at work. If you give yourself some time to slow down and consider where you want to end up both in your future, in your daily life, and with your mental health, then you will better be able to make a plan. For instance, a future goal would be to graduate college in the major of your choice. A daily goal is to stay sober and avoid all alcohol. Mental health goals would be to have the ability to answer the phone without having an anxiety attack.

Create S.M.A.R.T Goals

An acronym common for creating strong goals. S.M.A.R.T goals are specific, measurable, attainable, realistic, and time-sensitive.

Stay Specific

Specific so that you know exactly where you want to be and are less likely to fudge on the results. For instance, if your goal is to use cognitive behavioral therapy to treat your insomnia, the goal "sleep better" is unspecific. If you are currently only getting an average of four hours of sleep, then you can call five hours of sleep "better". Yet, this amount of sleep is still not enough. Try to create goals of where you specifically want to be. In this instance, it is scientifically shown that humans need between seven and eight hours of sleep. Therefore, a specific goal would be "get seven hours of sleep every night and wake up at the same time every day."

Have Measurable Goals

It is important to know whether or not you are making progress toward your goals. This may be harder to track with some things such as depression than it is in business. But there are still certain ways you can measure your progress. If you are someone with depression who finds yourself no longer wanting to get out of bed, then every day you don't struggle with getting out of bed is a progress. You tell by the frequency of your depression symptoms improving how close you are getting toward your goal.

Keep Them Attainable

When creating business and life goals, some people will create goals that are so high that they are unattainable. For instance, the goal of becoming a millionaire within five years of graduating from college isn't likely to be attained. Thankfully, goals for the purpose of cognitive behavioral therapy are much more likely to be attained. You have power over your thoughts. You can become sober. You can get to a place where you are happy. You can overcome your fears. Your insomnia can be cured. All of these goals and more are attainable.

However, goals such as "never have another anxiety attack" and "never feel depressed again" are examples of unattainable goals. Remember, cognitive behavioral therapy will take time and work. You can't expect your mental health to be cured overnight.

Stay Realistic

Similar to keeping your goals attainable is to keep them realistic. You are capable of more than you know. While it may at times feel impossible to overcome your struggles, you can do it. Many people have overcome the same struggles in the past and with the tools provided by CBT, you are able to overcome them as well. However, you also need to stay realistic and you can do this by forgiving yourself.

If you punish yourself for having anxiety, depression, insomnia, or any number of other problems, then you are only straying further away from your goal. Stay positive, forgive yourself, and keep pushing forward.

Time Matters

Having a time frame for when you want to have your goal completed can help you track your progress and help you act. This is because if we simply say "someday I want to have a better life," then we are less likely to make progress in order to reach that "someday." Although, if we say "I want to have the confidence to answer the phone within a year," not only can we track our progress, but we can stay encouraged to put in the work needed to attain the goal.

Lastly, remember that people are more likely to reach their goals when they share it with someone who supports them. You don't want to share it with someone who is negative, overbearing, and unlikely to support you. This is more likely to discourage you. Instead, find a family member or friend who you know frequently support you and are likely to help encourage you and hold you accountable. If you don't have someone like this in your life, you can always find a group of people locally or online. For instance, an alcoholic may join Alcoholics Anonymous. You may even be able to find social media groups such as those on Facbook of other people going through similar struggles. If you can find someone in these groups that you connect with, you can both encourage one another.

After we know the goals we hope to achieve through cognitive behavioral therapy, it is time to begin to solve our problems. We can do this by consistently tinkering with our situations, moods, and thoughts. We are not going to improve our mental health simply by thinking of it as one big project that somehow needs to get done. Instead, we need to work on individual aspects of our health, relationships, and situations. By adjusting these smaller aspects, we are able to work on and improve the whole.

For instance, when a college or professional football players are trying to improve their gameplay, the couch doesn't simply say "run further," "run faster," or "tackle better." Instead, the couch will give the players specific advice on how they can improve their gait when they run, how to improve their speed, and better ways to tackle successfully. By giving the players specific advice on specific problems, the couch is able to help the football players improve their overall ability.

Similarly, a professor wouldn't simply tell their students to study better or to improve their writing ability. Instead, a successful professor will walk their students through what exactly their students need to improve. They could show the students better resources to use and remind them that Wikipedia doesn't count as a source. If the student is struggling with spelling or grammar in their essays, the professor will point out exactly where the student is making mistake and give advice on what to do instead. By doing this, the professor is helping their students to improve exactly the way they need to, rather than giving ambiguous advice.

Similarly, you can use cognitive behavioral therapy to help you solve your individual problems and improve as a whole. You can achieve this by exploring your emotions and insecurities and then identifying the source of your problems and then finding solutions.

Cognitive behavioral therapy is known to be extremely beneficial and effective. However, the participants must be willing to put in effort and time to analyze their own thoughts and behaviors. This can be difficult, especially since people living with depression, anxiety, anger, or other emotional or mental issues are likely to dislike aspects of themselves. While nothing is wrong with them as a human being, these people may feel discouraged by looking at themselves honestly. But by working through this process, you can learn more about your internal state and how it can impact your outward behavior.

By learning to counteract your false and negative beliefs, you can replace them with positive and truthful beliefs. These can help improve a number of areas in life including all of your relationships, your work, sleep, and mental health.

For instance, people like Mary who are suffering from depression due to loss often develop a false belief that there is no point in communicating with others and that they can protect themselves by avoiding getting close to others. These people often also develop false ideas of their own worth, developing a negative self-esteem. As a result of these thoughts, these people often avoid social situations, begin to skip work or school when possible, and desire to do little else other than lying in bed.

We can use CBT in order to overcome these thoughts and behaviors. By using what is known as a functional analysis, we can gain a better understanding of our feelings, thoughts, and situations and how they impact our maladaptive behaviors. This isn't an easy process, especially for people who have a difficult time with introspection. But this process of developing a better sense of ourselves and gaining insight into our behavior is essential for improvement and treatment.

After developing a deeper understanding of ourselves, feelings, and thoughts, we are able to better focus on our behaviors. Due to our feelings and thoughts impacting our behaviors, we can create behavioral habits that only worsen our mental and emotional states. For instance, an addict will further believe that alcohol will make them feel better if they develop behavioral habits that support this false claim. Our feelings, thoughts, and behaviors can turn into a vicious cycle.

Thankfully, with cognitive behavioral therapy, we can learn practices that will help us overcome these behaviors and habits. We can learn to develop new habits, coping mechanisms, and plans to avoid falling back into our problematic behaviors. With CBT, we can make real change in our behaviors and prevent relapses. Whether you are trying to overcome depression or alcoholism, you can develop new behaviors that will help you better learn to cope and live a healthy and happy life.

You don't have to worry about making this change in behavior overnight. Your ingrained thoughts, emotions, and behaviors are not a light switch. You can't simply turn them off or on. But through a process of gradual steps to change these aspects, you can take steps toward your goal. Lydia could start by imagining herself in situations with dogs.

After she is able to do this well with plans on how to stay calm and in control of her emotions, she can move onto the next step. If some family or friends have friendly small dogs, she could try being around them while they are on a leash or in a kennel. Or she could even interact with puppies at an adoption event since puppies are much less frightening than a large full-grown dog.

As Lydia and other people utilizing CBT get more confident with each step, they can take the next one with more confidence. This gives the person security in seeing that they don't have to make a one-hundred and sixty-degree change overnight. They are also able to see their progress and learn that they can handle it.

In order to benefit from cognitive behavioral therapy, you need to work it into your daily life. After all, Mary, Lydia, and Matt will not improve if they only use the techniques they learn half of the time or even eighty percent of the time. It needs to be ingrained into your daily activities and mental state to make progress. Thankfully, there are some simple ways you can include CBT into your daily life and experience its many benefits.

Journal Throughout the Day

While by this point you already have a basic understanding of your thoughts and emotions, you need to stay on top of tracking them. A journal can help with this. Throughout the day, whenever you notice you are experiencing negative emotions or feelings track the following:

- Situation
- Mood
- Automatic Thoughts or Images
- Evidence that Supports my Thoughts
- Evidence that Disproves my Thoughts
- Alternative Healthy Thoughts
- New Mood

By journaling your situation, feelings, thoughts, and behaviors, you can gain a wider understanding of yourself. You may think that you already understand your triggers, feelings, and thoughts when you initially explored them as we described earlier. Yet, you will find that these can change over time and you may discover thoughts and behaviors you were previously ignorant of. By following through with journaling daily, you will be able to identify your emotions, insecurities, and the sources of your problems better so that you can take steps to further heal and improve.

Reconstruct your Cognition

Once we become aware of inaccurate or false ideas we hold on ourselves, behaviors, and the world, we can begin to learn why this false idea took root and why we began to believe it. This means that we can directly challenge these false ideas and replace them with the truth. For instance, a person who is in an accident and becomes disabled may develop the false idea that they are a shadow of their former selves and now are worth less than before. This can result in the person developing depression and anger at their situation.

But through cognitive behavioral therapy, they can learn to directly challenge this false belief of themselves. They can learn that these negative inaccurate thoughts are a result of ableism in society and not because of themselves. After they accept this, they can begin to see that they aren't a shadow of their former selves and they are still the same person. The abilities of their body have no impact on their worth as a human being.

Think it Over to Overcome it

People living with anxiety, fear, and obsessive-compulsive disorder (OCD) can greatly benefit from this technique. With this method, a person follows through with a thought experiment, in which they imagine a situation that they are uncomfortable with. Imagine the worst case scenario that could happen. Allow the event to play through in your mind and then realize that even if the worst happened, it is likely to turn out okay. This method can also help people realize that the worst case scenario is unlikely and even if it did happen, they can make plans to handle it. Doing this takes the fear out of the situation and gives you the control over your fear.

Exposure Therapy

If you have a difficult time going to a specific place, interacting with people, or exposing yourself to other experiences, it is beneficial to expose yourself to it while you focus on staying calm. This means that if Lydia is interacting with dogs, she can remind herself of truthful thoughts and use coping mechanisms to stay calm. Mary can practice exposing herself to her loved ones without withdrawing due to her depression. Matt can learn to interact with people who often make him angry, while still controlling his temper. This type of therapy that goes along with CBT can especially be helpful for people who suffer from anxiety of obsessive-compulsive disorder.

It can be especially beneficial to journal during these situations, as it will help you refrain from the behavior you are trying to overcome. It can also help you to remind yourself of the truth rather than the lies that your brain is conditioned to believe.

It is important to expose ourselves to something that we fear or are uncomfortable with in order to overcome it.

Progressive Muscle Relaxation

This method, also known as PMR, should be familiar with people who practice meditation or mindfulness. With this technique, a person practices relaxing one group of muscles at a time until their entire body is relaxed. This can be completed on your own, with audio assistance, or even a smartphone app instructing you. Multiple studies have revealed the benefits of this practice. These studies have revealed that PMR has the ability to help decrease stress in mind and body more than other forms of relaxation. It has even been found to lower heart rate, reduce the cortisol hormone which increases stress, treats anxiety, and can even help improve the quality of life of cancer patients.

Breathe In and Out

Similarly to PMR, breathing techniques should be familiar to people who have used mindfulness or meditation. By utilizing regular, mathematics, and deep breathing exercises, a person can feel a sense of calm. This can allow them to find mental balance and more easily look at their situation and thoughts more clearly, accurately, and rationally.

The American Institute of Stress even explains that while many people will rest in front of the TV after a long and difficult day, this does little to relieve stress. The result is a buildup of stress over time, which impacts both our mental and physical health. In order to fight back against this daily stress, we need to utilize our body's natural ability to go into a state of relaxation.

This is known as the "relaxation response" and results in lowered blood pressure, decreased heart rate, relaxed muscle tension, improved oxygen delivery to the cells, an increase in the feel-good endorphins, detoxification of harmful chemicals and toxins, and of course decreased stress.

Our stress in life builds up, which can impact our mental health. This especially affects people with illnesses such as depression, obsessive-compulsive disorder, anxiety, panic disorder, alcoholism, insomnia, and much more! We need to deal with this stress both mentally and physically in order to lessen these problems. By utilizing deep breathing, your body can go into the relaxation response, physically allowing your body to remove stress and relax. But this process also helps to clear your mind and can help you further along in cognitive behavioral therapy.

When we are in a stressed or disturbed state of mind, our situation seems worse than it actually is. This will affect our emotions, thoughts, and behavior. But by utilizing deep breathing and the other techniques mentioned here, you can find a state of calm in both mind and body. This will allow you to correct the false ideas in your mind, find the truth, and calmly figure out solutions to any problems you may be experiencing.

It is important to remember that it is not the events that happen to us that control us, rather the meaning we allow them to hold over us. If we allow these events to control our emotions, thoughts, and behaviors, we can begin to believe the false negative thoughts as truth.

Just like Mary believes that there is no point in interacting with other people because they may die. Or how Mary believes that she is worth less than other people. While these thoughts may have been small when they first began, as time went on, these thoughts grew and took control. This turns her feelings, thoughts, and behaviors into a vicious cycle that reinforce one another.

But if Mary learns to take control of these feelings, thoughts, and behaviors through cognitive behavioral therapy, then they will lose their power over her. She may still struggle with these thoughts at first or from time to time, but gradually she will come to see them as false. The more consistently Mary journals, interact with other people, practices muscle relaxation and deep breathing, and visualizes day is going well, then the more confidence she will have in herself and the truth. She will learn to believe that she does have worth and that while no living thing can continue to live forever, there is still meaning in connections and interacting with others. She can begin to enjoy and love life again the more she fights back against the dysfunctional thought processes brought on by depression.

Through this process, we can overcome our automatic thoughts that tell us lies such as *"I completely failed," "I can't do this,"* and *"Nobody likes me.*

But even if you aren't someone who is living with a major depressive disorder, anxiety, disorder, or a number of other disorders, you can still benefit from cognitive behavioral therapy. In fact, this type of therapy can help anyone in their daily lives. Whether you struggle with self-acceptance, low self-esteem, or anger management on a daily basis or only occasionally, CBT can help you develop better thought processes, coping mechanisms, and behaviors.

Improve Your Self-Esteem

How we think about ourselves affects every area of our lives. Our confidence, feelings, thoughts, and behaviors can all be impacted by what we think of ourselves. A person with a healthy self-esteem can accurately judge their abilities, how those around them feel, and can regulate their emotions and thoughts accordingly. On the other hand, someone with low self-esteem is likely to be highly critical of themselves, incorrectly believe that the people around them must dislike them, and they are less likely to act on positive opportunities. However, cognitive behavioral therapy has been studied extensively for self-esteem and it has been found to be the most effective type of treatment.

For treating self-esteem, CBT can help us recognize the negative and false thinking habits we fall into and replace them with positive truthful thoughts. By replacing our distorted ideas of ourselves with truthful ideas, we can learn to see that we have value, that we aren't a failure, and that there are people out there who genuinely like and care for us.

When a person has low self-esteem, they are likely to avoid activities that they feel they may fail at. This means that they could avoid social interactions, higher education, a challenging job, or even a simple hobby. This results in the person having fewer rewarding experiences and can lead to depression. By learning to alter behavior and re-engage in these activities, you can break the cycle and learn to fully enjoy activities. You don't have to be perfect for an experience to be worthwhile, valuable, and enjoyable.

People with self-esteem issues often have little assertiveness. Training to increase assertiveness can be combined with cognitive behavioral therapy. This will help a person make their feelings and requests known better, and in the process, they can begin to feel their own importance rather than worthlessness.

These same people often struggle with feeling helpless and powerless in situations. But with thinking over situations before they happen and utilizing problem-solving technique, they can learn how to overcome their struggles. This can give the person a boost of encouragement and a further sense of self-agency. By creating a plan ahead, you will not have to be stressed at the moment when something occurs.

If someone struggles with social skills due to their low self-esteem, they can learn to practice. Rather than avoiding situations, throw yourself into them with people that you feel comfortable with. As you learn more social skills, you can begin to interact with a wider range of people. This will continue to boost your confidence while increasing your ability to interact with others.

Increase Your Self-Acceptance

While a lack of self-acceptance and self-esteem often go hand in hand and can be treated similarly, there are slight differences. Self-esteem is often a person having a disbelief in their abilities, whereas, self-acceptance is often a person struggling to accept their thoughts and mental state.

Cognitive behavioral therapy can be used to help patients to stop denying, avoiding, and struggling with their emotions. Instead, they can learn to accept their feelings and find appropriate ways in which to react to them. When a person begins to accept what they feel, deal with the emotions, they can then move forward in life. This is especially helpful for people who live with mental illness or who are overcoming trauma.

By working with a psychologist, they can listen to you and help you learn how to process your emotions in a healthy manner, accept them, and move on. This can help you to improve your relationships, find joy in being yourself, and overcome traumatic life events. You can also practice this to an extent on your own by using the emotional thought journal method we have taught you. This method can help you learn which emotions and thoughts are true and which are not. This is extremely important because by suppressing our emotions, we gradually develop more stress and harmful beliefs.

Once you make a commitment to accept yourself, then you can face any issues you are facing, become more confident, increase your optimism, overcome your past, and create new behaviors that are based on truth, acceptance, and your personal goals.

Manage Your Anger

Everyone experiences anger to some degree. However, some people experience it more frequently or in outbursts. This is one of the problems that Matt deals with. While Matt is generally well-liked and enjoys a vibrant social life, sometimes he feels as if he can't control his anger. When he feels disrespected or criticized, then that turns all around him red and he practically explodes. When Matt gets angry, everyone around him knows it, whether he is at home or in a restaurant.

But with cognitive behavioral therapy, you can target your anger and the thoughts and behaviors that are tied to it. As you progress with using CBT, you can find that your anger gradually decreases, your periods of anger last for a shorter period of time, you feel it more mildly, and you will gain control over your emotions, thoughts, and behaviors.

If you are struggling to overcome your anger, then you can rate its strength, frequency, and duration in your CBT journal. From a zero to one-hundred, meaningless to more, rate how strongly you feel your anger, how frequently, and how long it lasts. During the beginning, you may need to track this daily. But the later you get in your journey and learn to overcome your anger, you can begin to track it less frequently.

Everyone can get angry over different events. While one person may get angry about being interrupted, another may patiently wait to continue what they had been saying. This is often because our anger can be based on our past. If we have a history of being treated poorly or abused, then those situations in the future are more likely to cause us to become defensive.

This is because anger often goes along with the subconscious belief that we can protect ourselves from harm, abuse, or mistreatment if we confront the person, action, or circumstance that is upsetting us.

To help you better understand your anger and the reasons behind it, remember a recent circumstance when you were angry and journal it. If you are unable to accurately recall what happened, journal your anger the next time it occurs. First, journal the strength, frequency, and duration, then journal the situation, mood, automatic thoughts or images, evidence that supports your thoughts, evidence that disproves your thoughts, alternative healthy thoughts, and your new mood after the evaluation.

By logging this, you can learn what was going through your mind when you were angry and develop a new understanding of yourself. This will allow you to better manage or express your anger and learn more constructive ways to manage it.

Chapter 4: Cognitive Behavioral Therapy in Action

By this point, you know well how to utilize cognitive behavioral therapy in general circumstances. But you may want more detail on how to find the most benefit if you are living with a specific condition. This is because CBT is not a single method. Rather, it is a combination of many techniques that can be altered depending on the condition that is being treated. In this chapter, we will go over how you can use CBT to help with panic disorder, insomnia, bipolar disorder, obsessive-compulsive disorder, self-harm, post-traumatic stress disorder, and more. Combining the tips in this chapter with the basic elements of CBT will help you get the most out of your treatment and find relief.

Insomnia

Sleep medication is a common treatment for short-term bouts of insomnia. This can be especially helpful for people who are going through a period of grief or high stress. But the options for people with long-term chronic insomnia are limited. There may be some newer medications, but these are ineffective on many people. They can also cause it so that people become unable to sleep without relying on the prescription.

But cognitive behavioral therapy is an approved treatment for the treatment of insomnia and has been shown to be highly effective. If you are worried about side effects of medication, becoming dependent, or unable to find a medication that works for you, then CBT may be the answer you are looking for.

Unlike prescriptions, CBT can help to address the cause of insomnia, rather than masking the symptoms. Although people with especially difficult cases of insomnia may benefit from a combination of both prescriptions and CBT.

It is important to remember that cognitive behavioral therapy isn't an overnight fix. This is a process and does take both time and effort.

Professional cognitive behavioral therapy involves regular visits with a trained psychologist who can customize your treatment plan. They will do this by assessing your sleep habits through a journal that you keep.

A U.S. Navy swim and safety instructor, Caroline developed a terrible case of insomnia while recovering from a knee surgery. The pain of her knee was excruciating, which led to her requiring medication that made her sleepy. Between the sleepiness from the pain medication and doctors' orders to stay in bed, Caroline found it difficult to stay awake throughout the day without drifting off to sleep. Yet, these naps greatly impacted her sleep schedule.

Before long, Caroline found that it was nearly impossible to fall asleep and stay asleep at nighttime. Even after her knee was healed and she was able to go back to working with the Navy, Caroline could not stop napping during the day. Every day as soon as she got home from work, she would fall asleep. This led to her being unable to sleep soundly throughout the night and continued to leave her exhausted in a brutal cycle.

After trying a variety of prescription sleep aids, Caroline found that none of them helped her except for Ambien. Finally, she was no longer feeling fatigued and sleepy at work and she was able to sleep through the night! Despite this, Caroline knew that she couldn't stay on the medication for the remainder of her life. This was soon proven when her insurance would no longer cover the Ambien. This is because it is a medication specifically for short-term use, therefore, the insurance provider would not approve it for a long-term case of insomnia.

Caroline was soon recommended to the Clinical Assistant Professor in the Department of Psychiatry at Brown Medical School, who was also a Director of Behavioral Sleep Medicine in Rhode Island. While she was hesitant to see a psychiatrist, Caroline knew she had to do something so she set up an appointment with Dr. Donn Posner.

Caroline still learned that cognitive behavioral therapy wasn't an overnight easy cure. Instead, she found that the first six weeks of treatment, she was getting very little sleep. But after she kept a sleeping journal, Dr. Posner was able to review it and help Caroline find how to cure her insomnia.

It wasn't easy, but Caroline learned that she had to completely stop taking naps and couldn't go to bed early any longer. In fact, she wasn't allowed to go to bed until midnight. Without her early evening bedtime and naps, Caroline was finding it incredibly difficult to stay awake until her bedtime. It was the hardest six weeks of her life. Thankfully, Caroline soon started to sleep better and as she did, she was allowed to back up her bedtime so that she wasn't going to sleep as late.

By looking over Caroline's sleep journal over the following weeks, Dr. Posner was able to further customize her sleep routine to help lessen her insomnia. He found that using stimulus control was important. With this portion of CBT for insomnia, he found that she needed to spend less time in her bedroom when she wasn't sleeping. This even means that if Caroline found she was unable to fall asleep, that she was supposed to leave her bedroom and not come back until she felt that she was ready to sleep.

She was also supposed to practice better sleep hygiene. This entailed Caroline having to avoid stimulants such as caffeine, alcohol, and tobacco before bedtime, as well as avoiding exercise close to bedtime and sleeping in a cool and completely dark room.

Professionals can find many problems that an individual may not recognize their sleep routine. For instance, Caroline was a frequent offender of clock watching. Many people who suffer from insomnia will begin to stare at the clock at night, watching the hours tick by. But this is dangerous because it becomes a part of your routine. Even worse, it leads to frustration and worry which are only known to worsen insomnia.

Caroline was instructed by Dr. Posner to completely stop looking at her clock after going to bed. Therefore, she covered her clocks in her room so that she could still be woken by the alarm, but couldn't see the time.

Another task that Caroline was given by Dr. Posner was to stop working close to bedtime. This only wakes up the brain, when it should be settling down for bedtime. She was also told to avoid watching TV in the evening as that has a similar effect. Caroline stopped bringing her work home with her in the evening. Instead, she would spend her time relaxing with a book or painting.

After six weeks of working through insomnia-specific cognitive behavioral therapy, Caroline found that her sleep had greatly improved and was only continuing to get better. While she originally needed to see Dr. Posner on a weekly basis, she now only rarely has checkup appointments although she is staying on top of relapse prevention care. With this, Caroline can ensure that she sticks to the cognitive behavioral therapy tactics she was taught and prevent another bout of insomnia.

Caroline does this by not compensating for the loss of sleep, beginning her sleep restriction phase if she finds she has insomnia for more than a few days, and avoiding stimulating substances and activities before bed.

Cognitive behavioral therapy can also help you to eliminate negative worries and thoughts that might keep you lying awake all night. This is one of the most common causes of insomnia. Because of this, CBT targets the direct reason that you are unable to sleep. Following is a list and description of the most common CBT treatment options for insomnia.

Relaxation Training

The use of meditation, muscle relaxation, visualization, and other relaxation techniques to calm or overcome negative thinking. This can be practiced throughout the day as well to help relieve anxiety, which will naturally lessen it at night as well.

Stimulus Therapy

There are many factors in our lives that can make our mind avoid sleep. This can include the time we spend in our room, the naps we take, and what time we get up in the morning. As an example, it is often recommended to limit bedroom activity to sex and sleep. Similarly, only go to bed when you are tired and if you are unable to fall asleep within twenty minutes, then go to another room until you feel you are able to sleep. Try to get out of bed at the same time every day and try to greatly limit naps.

Sleep Hygiene

This process involves limiting lifestyle factors that interfere with sleep. You will want to either avoid stimulants within a few hours of bedtime or avoid them completely. Some people may be unable to sleep without a bedtime snack and that's okay. Try to engage in relaxing activities such as reading, writing, listening to calming music, painting, or taking a bath before bed.

It is imperative to avoid working, watching TV, doing the computer, exercising, and other stimulating activities before bed.

Paradoxical Inattention

Also known as remaining passively awake, this process involves a person resting while avoiding trying to sleep. This is because when we are actively trying to sleep, we can become anxious and worry, which only worsens insomnia. Instead, it is important to be able to lie in bed without actively trying to sleep. Don't worry, the sleep will come on its own, you can't make it happen.

Biofeedback

Often used alongside relaxation training, biofeedback is more complex than the other methods.

However, it can be highly successful. With this method, a person is given a device that can detect brainwave frequency, muscle tension, and other biological aspects. With biofeedback, you are taught how to adjust your own brain waves, blood pressure, muscle tension, heart rate, and body temperature.

It may take some practice and concentration, but some people find that within only a few sessions they are able to get the hang of it. Using this method, you can directly impact various body functions in order to help your body be in a state where it can more easily fall asleep.

There are many components involved in cognitive behavioral therapy for insomnia. Although many people don't use all of these components, you may combine several of them to take control of your sleep and health.

Anxiety

Throughout this book, we have frequently discussed how we need to replace our false thoughts with thoughts of truth. This is especially important with people living with one of a number of anxiety disorders. Often, people with these disorders need to learn to let go of guilt, embarrassment, and anger over their pasts. How to be more realistic and not hold themselves to perfection, how to overcome misconceptions they may have about their self-worth and abilities, how to deal with procrastination, and how to become more assertive when needed.

This is especially needed with anxiety disorders because people with anxiety have developed automatic thoughts that are negative and inaccurate from reality. These thoughts only increase anxiety and lessen their ability to cope with life.

If you are someone living with an anxiety disorder, you have most likely heard someone simply tell you to "think more positively." Sadly, you know that it isn't that easy. If it were, you would have resolved your problems long ago. Instead, your brain is in a constant state of anxiety and negativity that is difficult to overcome. Just telling yourself to be less anxious and trying to think of something else doesn't resolve the problem of your brain.

But with practice and commitment, you can use cognitive behavioral therapy to retrain your brain. While at first, this may simply mean that when you notice a negative thought, you analyze it and turn it into a realistic positive or neutral thought, over time it can become more powerful and easier.

As the process becomes easier, you can continue to challenge more difficult thoughts until this feels like second nature. Gradually, your neural pathways and memory processes will physically alter. This will naturally lead you to feel different.

You will find that it is easier to be optimistic, you will find yourself anxious less often, and anxiety will be easier to overcome. It takes patience and consistency, but it is well worth it.

Systematic desensitization is one of the most common types of treatment used in cognitive behavioral therapy for anxiety disorders. This type of CBT treatment involves a person gradually exposing themselves to situations which often cause anxiety. Over time, the person will learn to cope. These situations will begin to affect the person less and they can even move onto more difficult anxiety challenges. This process is scary at first, but it isn't as simple as facing your fears and toughening up. Instead, you work on very gradually working through a step-by-step process.

For instance, if someone is afraid of heights, they wouldn't immediately begin by bungee jumping off of a cliff to face their fears. This would only worsen their fear and make it more difficult to overcome. Instead, a trained therapy, psychologist or psychiatrist can help you work through these fears at a pace that is right for you.

This type of therapy often begins with visualization. A person with a phobia of heights can begin by imagining themselves in a situation that would usually frighten them. As imagining these situations becomes easier, they can very slowly begin to transition the therapy to real-world applications.

Although this must be done very slowly to prevent the process from backfiring. This means a person with a fear of heights would most likely try standing on a short footstool or going onto the second story of a building.

If someone is unable to make appointments to a psychologist either due to logistics or their own anxiety, there are still options to work with a trained professional. In recent years,

CBT over the internet has become increasingly popular. Research has even found that it can be highly successful and is more suited to online use than other forms of therapy.

If you have an anxiety disorder and hope to use cognitive behavioral therapy for treatment, there are a few key factors to attain success. Studies show how successful CBT can largely rely on the individual and their willingness to confront uncomfortable or difficult thoughts and complete homework projects. It may be daunting, but CBT has been shown to be highly effective in people with anxiety if they are willing to work for it. Thankfully, the results have been shown to be well worth the work that they require and are long-lasting.

Panic Disorder
Some people may assume that anxiety disorders and panic disorder are the same things. But while they can both become debilitating, they are different. The best way to describe this is that anxiety is the type of fear that you experience when you are worried that you are going to fail a class in college and will have to repeat a year. Whereas panic attacks are the type of fear you would experience if someone is breaking into your house and you are in imminent danger.
Yet, panic disorders happen when there is no present danger. They can be triggered by something as small as someone touching your arm. Everyone's panic attack triggers vary. They are usually accompanied by a variety of physical symptoms. These can include dizziness, shortness of breath, a racing heart rate, feeling faint, trembling, nausea, chills or hot flashes, chest pain, choking sensations, or sweating. They can also make people feel as if they are dying, a feeling of detachment, or as if they are going crazy.

These attacks are sudden and usually last between one and ten minutes. The person experiences a strong urge to run away and reach safety due to our natural flight or fight response. At first, these attacks often are triggered by no known cause, but over time, they can become isolated to certain situations. For instance, a person may develop panic attacks due to flying, elevators, leaving home, or a number of other situations. If left untreated, they can often result in anxiety or a reliance on drugs or alcohol to ease the symptoms. Many people become disabled due to panic attacks and are no longer able to manage to work.

There has been significant research proving the effectiveness of CBT on panic disorder. In fact, after twelve weeks of thirteen small group sessions participants improved greatly. Comprehensive assessments were conducted on all participants both prior to therapy, midway, and once it was completed. By the end of the twelve weeks, every one of the participants was free of their spontaneous panic attacks and was able to qualify as high functioning. This type of therapy has been shown to greatly outperform other treatment methods including medication.

The CBT treatment plans for panic disorder often involve mindfulness, exposure therapy, relaxation training, cognitive restructuring to replace anxiety-provoking thoughts with more balanced thoughts, and stress reduction to help a person learn to react to situations more calmly.

Depression and Suicidal Ideation

Life has many ups and downs that can lead people to develop a case of depression. As many as fourteen million adults in America suffer from a major depressive disorder at some point in their lives. While for some people this is only a temporary problem, other's struggle with depression for their entire lives. This can make people feel lonely, hopeless, and empty. But there is no need to suffer silently. There is always someone who can help you, whether it is a family member, friend, someone online, or a psychologist.

While depression can become disabling and even lead to suicidal ideation (which means thoughts of suicide) or attempted suicide, CBT has been shown to be an effective treatment. Whether you are suffering from moderate or severe depression, cognitive behavioral therapy has been shown time and again to be successful in treatment. This therapy can either be done as the sole method of treatment or combined with anti-depressants.

When treating depression, your therapist will focus on helping you to overcome your negative thought processes and changing them to something more balanced. This takes time, but over time it can change your brain's shape and synapses, not only mentally helping your brain improve, but physically aiding it as well.

Addictions and Obsessions
Whether you are suffering from drug or alcohol addiction, cognitive behavioral therapy can help. It may seem overwhelming, but with the process of CBT, an overwhelming problem can be turned into small manageable pieces. A therapist or psychologist will have the ability to analyze you personally along with your situation, difficulties, and other problems. Your therapy plan can be customized so that it is approachable and while still helpful both in the short-term and long-term.

Just like with other forms of CBT, people using it for alcohol or drug addiction will be asked to practice homework. This homework is most often the process of analyzing your own thoughts and feelings and turning false negative thoughts into balanced thoughts.

There are three main factors that are frequently focused on this form of CBT. These are recognizing, avoiding, and coping.

Your psychologist will help you learn to recognize the instances that you are most likely to indulge your addiction.

You will then learn to avoid these situations when it is appropriate or feasible.

Lastly, you will learn to cope with a wide range of behaviors caused by addiction. You can be taught how to find better self-control, explore the positive and negative effects of your addiction, monitor yourself to recognize cravings and weaknesses early on, and how to develop strategies for when you are most likely to engage in your addiction.

Addiction can be overwhelming and feel as if it is impossible to overcome. Although, research clearly shows the benefits of cognitive behavioral therapy in the treatment of both alcohol and drug addiction. In fact, the skills and benefits people learn from CBT have been shown to remain long after the participants finish their therapy.

Obsessive-Compulsive Disorder

Obsessive-compulsive disorder, otherwise known as OCD, is often thought to simply be people who are prone to cleaning or organizing. However, someone simply being picky when it comes to organization or cleaning is completely different from the level of obsessiveness that OCD causes.

Firstly, OCD does not mean someone tends to clean or organize. Some people may, but there are many other ways in which OCD may manifest. OCD is characterized by persistent and repeated unwanted thoughts. Even if a person tries to ignore them, they often are unable to. This can lead to rituals or behaviors that are compulsive. These compulsions may be so overwhelming that a person who feels the need to wash their hands may end up washing them until they are raw and bleeding on a daily basis.

Some of the common obsessions with OCD include thoughts of harm coming to you, worry that you may harm someone else, aggressive impulses, unwanted sexual thoughts, fear of contamination, and needing things orderly or symmetrical.

Thankfully, cognitive behavioral therapy has been shown to be one of the most effective forms of treatment of OCD. The research has shown that a significant seventy-five percent of patients with OCD improve greatly from CBT and some studies even have the number as high as eighty percent. Due to the success of CBT with few side effects or negative aspects, it has been chosen as the top choice for managing OCD by the Center for Anxiety Disorders and Trauma, the National Institute for Health and Clinical Excellence, and other originations.

When first beginning therapy, a person will be asked to list and describe their various compulsions and obsessions. They will rank them so that the therapist can easily see what is most difficult for each individual. Next, they will be asked to give recent examples of when their OCD was more severe. It is important to go into detail of the thoughts, images, urges, and doubts that may have occurred during that time.

The goal of cognitive behavioral therapy isn't to get rid of the thoughts that occur alongside OCD. Instead, a therapist can help you learn to cope with them. They can help overturn these urges and thoughts so that they no longer control them or frighten them. The thoughts that once used to control their life will turn into ideal passing. They will no longer have to act on them in order to feel relief.

A good therapist or psychologist is able to learn how an individual's OCD works, what keeps it going, the ideas behind it, and how to change it into something manageable. The treatment of OCD may not be easy, no matter what type of therapy a person chooses. But, with cognitive behavioral therapy and a well-trained professional, it is possible to find relief.

Eating Disorders and Negative Body Image

Whether you live with anorexia, bulimia, binge eating, or another eating disorder, cognitive behavioral therapy may help. In fact, out of all the uses for CBT, eating disorders have been shown to be one of the most effective cases for this type of treatment and therapy. Largely because CBT focuses both on the mental and physical aspects of eating disorders. CBT does not only help treat one type of eating disorder, as it has been found to help all types.

In therapy, people will be taught both how their cognition affects their body image, self-evaluation, self-worth, perfectionism, and core beliefs. They will also be taught how to manage the behavioral factors of eating disorders such as purging, binge-eating, self-harm, weighing, and other actions.

A therapist or psychologist can help educate you to help you learn the skills and education you need in order to gain a more balanced understanding of yourself. There are three main phases — the behavioral, the cognitive, and the maintenance.

During the behavioral phase, the therapist can help you to balance your eating and eliminate your individual symptoms based on your specific eating disorder. Although a person's emotions often worsen during this portion of the therapy, a therapist can help. By teaching you coping mechanisms, strategies, and important tools to manage your feelings both in sessions and at home, your psychologist can help you move onto the next phase of treatment.

During the cognitive phase, the psychologist will focus on changing your thought patterns. By identifying and targeting harmful and negative thoughts such as "I can only be happy if I lose weight," you can gain a new understanding and lessen your desires to continue in the harmful behavior. Your negative thoughts can be replaced with balanced alternatives such as "my worth is not dependent on my size or the number on the scale."

Once you begin the maintenance phase, your psychologist will focus on helping you reduce known triggers, the prevention of relapses, and teach you tools to maintain your hard-earned progress.

Post-Traumatic Stress Disorder

"One of the key factors that allow CBT to be one of the most effective theories when working with clients with PTSD is its ability to focus on processing thoughts, beliefs, and emotions about individual activating events. The ABC model allows the client to isolate the traumatic event and begin to dispute maladaptive thoughts, emotions, and behaviors associated with that event without being overwhelmed with other life events." - Felicia Jessup, M.A, NCC, LPC

Everyone will experience stressful and upsetting events during their lifetime. But when these events are especially upsetting or stressful, they may turn into a traumatic experience which is incredibly distressing. The loss of a loved one, an intense surgery, an armed robbery, all of these events and more can be traumatic.

When situations are especially horrific, dangerous, or lead to a sense of helplessness, then a person may develop a long-term psychological scar. This can be caused by a wide variety of situations, but some of the most common include abuse, sexual assault, war experience, victimization from a crime, serious injury, and natural disasters.

While it cannot be predicted who will develop PTSD, those who suffer worse trauma are more likely to develop this condition. Nobody is immune to mental health conditions, PTSD, or otherwise.

There are multiple theories on PTSD and understanding these theories can help during the treatment process. The emotional processing theory by Rauch and Foa from 2006 suggests that people who have experienced trauma may develop unhealthy associations due to the experience. This can cause the person to develop further stress when they encounter something that reminds them of the experience. These same people may also develop maladaptive cognition and distorted views.

Thankfully, with the use of the cognitive model that we have previously discussed, also known as the ABC model, along with exposure therapy conducted by a trained professional, many people are able to find relief.

A therapist may use a variety of elements found within cognitive behavioral therapy to help their patients with PTSD. Although, just as the quote by Ms. Felicia Jessup mentions, one of the most successful components of CBT is its ability to focus on a person's thoughts, beliefs, and emotions about the traumatic event. Ms. Jessup utilized this method frequently while working as a civilian military liaison for the U.S Air Force. She would use the cognitive model or ABC model to help her patients identify and re-evaluate their unhealthy thinking patterns or distortions. These thoughts such as expecting catastrophic events, negative thinking that overrides positive thinking, and self-blame for the traumatic event can be re-conceptualized. This allows the patient to gain a better understanding, not only of the traumatic event but also of themselves and their ability to cope.

Within cognitive behavioral therapy, a therapist can slowly help a patient work through exposure therapy. This is done in a safe environment and with the patient's full consent, so as to not cause further trauma. By exposing the patient to reminders of their trauma, whether through visualization, sounds, or other methods in a controlled environment, they are able to heal. This process can give the patient increased self-confidence and they can learn to reduce the need to avoid or escape similar reminders.

By helping a patient learn about how trauma may affect them, relaxation techniques for managing stress, and planning solutions for uncomfortable or triggering situations, a therapist can further improve a patient's control, confidence, and healing.

Chapter 5: Dialectical Behavioral Therapy in Action

If you previously heard of CBT prior to picking up this book, then you might have heard of DBT or dialectical behavioral therapy as well. But what does the term 'dialectical' even mean? This term is defined as two opinions or forces that may appear to be opposites working together synergistically.

This means that while both acceptance and change may seem to be opposites, in DBT a patient is taught both to accept themselves where they are at and to change so that they may attain their goals. This method was developed by Marsha Linehan Ph.D., ABPP, and uses elements of emotional regulation, mindfulness, interpersonal effectiveness, and distress tolerance. The goal of this therapy is to help patients create goals, build a life that they feel is worthwhile in living, and decrease harmful behaviors.

While this treatment was originally created for people who are suicidal and diagnosed with borderline personality disorder (BPD), it has been found to be beneficial for many other individuals as well. The four elements of DBT in detail include:

- Emotional Regulation: The ability to reduce painful emotions and vulnerability while changing the emotions that you desire.

- Mindfulness: The practice of learning to be fully present and aware during the moment.

- Interpersonal Effectiveness: Begin to ask other for what you need and also learn the ability to say 'no' when needed while still retaining solid relationships with others.

- Distress Tolerance: Learn that you don't have to change painful situations, rather learn how to tolerate them.

These elements of DBT are usually taught in four different methods which include skills training group, personalized treatment, phone coaching, and team consultation.

The skills training group in DBT is centered on helping the patients learn behavioral skills. These training groups meet once weekly for a twenty-four week period and may even sometimes be repeated for a full year of training. During this time, groups function similarly to a class and the participants are given homework to help them integrate their newly learned skills during daily life.

While the participants are already done a once-weekly group training session, they will also attend a once-weekly therapy session. The purpose of this is to increase the patient's motivation, set specific goals, and help them further apply the skills they learned in the group.

Between sessions of individual therapy, the patients are able to contact their therapist on the phone for immediate help. This is especially influential in people who live with incredibly difficult diagnoses that are obstructing their daily lives.

The team consultation portion is meant to help the therapists and to support them with patients who may have increasingly complex and difficult to treat conditions. This team of people helps the therapist to stay motivated and may give advice when needed. The team consultation group typically will meet once weekly.

The therapist will organize the patient's care into four stages and these stages are based on the individual person's timeline and behavior. Rather than having a set period of time for each stage, this gives the therapist the ability to spend as much or little time within a stage as the patient requires.

The first stage is when a patient first begins DBT and because of this, they often describe their mental state as "hell". They may even try to self-harm, attempt suicide, or use alcohol or drugs. This stage ends when the patient is no longer self-destructive and begins to show control of their behavior.

During the second stage, the patient may no longer be an immediate danger to themselves. Although, they continue to suffer and feel as if they are living in quiet desperation. The second stage ends once the patient is able to move on from quiet desperation and begins to experience emotions fully.

The third stage comprises of the patients learning to create goals, find peace, build a sense of self-respect, and experience joy. The goal for this stage is that the patient is able to happily live a life of both happiness and unhappiness.

Stage four is for people who are looking for a deeper spiritual meaning in their lives. This stage creates a deeper sense of fulfillment for people who are unable to settle into a life of regular ups and downs that come and go throughout life. The goal of this stage is to help patients move on from feeling incomplete to experiencing a fulfilled sense of joy and freedom.

Why are we talking about DBT in an book focusing on CBT? Well, because dialectical behavioral therapy was created based off of CBT. When Dr. Linehan and other therapists first created this form of therapy, they included many CBT techniques. This includes homework, behavioral analysis, skills training, and a behavioral rating scale. They created this because some patients who struggle with the need to change and becoming overwhelmed didn't feel as if their needs were being met. But after Dr. Linehan and the other therapists looked over video recordings of their sessions, they noticed similarities in what helped these struggling patients. These patients required a plan that helped them learn to manage their pain and find purpose in living. After beginning the new therapy method, these patients continued on with therapy, improved more quickly, and their relationship with their therapists improved.

Therefore, DBT has many of the same benefits of cognitive behavioral therapy. Although, if a person finds that CBT isn't enough for their mental health needs, then they may need to try dialectical behavioral therapy.

A psychologist who trained under Dr. Linehan learns how to effectively use DBT. Dr. Kelly Koerner encourages people to use aspects of cognitive and dialectical behavioral therapies in their daily lives. One instance they recommend using these therapies in is when we are stuck between two opinions or courses of action. This could mean that if you are struggling with a circumstance, but you are unable to change it, the techniques of DBT can help. You can find a way to either accept or change the circumstance.

During a lecture for the National Education Alliance for Borderline Personality Disorder, Dr. Koerner discussed how these techniques can be integrated into daily life. As she discussed how DBT can help people, she led the listeners through the process of using it.

- Identify the two competing positions. This will vary from person to person, but for instance, say the positions are to either adopt a dog or adopt a cat.
- Fully examine both positions in an honest and straightforward manner. You want to make a list of what the pros or the truths of both sides.
- Focus on your body, find your center of gravity, and focus on deep slow breathing. Do this until you have developed a calm and grounded feeling of balance.

- Honestly ask yourself what your purpose in life is and how the person who you want to be would rectify or decide on the situation. What matters most to you? Years down the road when you are older, how will you feel about your choice? Focus on keeping grounded in these thoughts.

- While staying grounded, allow yourself to examine your feelings and all of the truths regarding your dilemma. We have all been shaped by our environment and how we were raised and this affects our opinions. Consider the person from the opposing opinion, how they formed their opinion, and what may be shaping it.

- In order to see what all led to the conflict, create a chain analysis. This can show all the ongoing emotions such as anger, jealousy, or disappointment. Although, it can also show other emotions that led up to the forming of opinions such as compassion, empathy, generosity, and kindness.

- Finally, you can end by verbally validating both positions while fleshing out possible solutions for each side. When dealing with conflict, you should try to combine the solutions so that it is a compromise for both people.

Dr. Koerner stresses that even if we are unable to see a solution immediately, we can still learn to accept the circumstance. We can focus on demonstrating compassion.

Anxiety

Our emotions are vital in the way our lives function. Yet, while emotions such as fear can be helpful when we are in a time of danger, sometimes we may develop anxiety disorders where these emotions are caused by unknown triggers. This anxiety, rather than helping us to survive in a dangerous situation, simply makes life into a miserable challenge. Even if we try to simply "think happy thoughts," the anxiety won't go away.

Thankfully, with dialectical behavioral therapy, we can learn cognitive and emotional skills which we can then apply to our lives. Even if our emotions are incredibly difficult and distressing, DBT is equipped to handle them. By working your way through DBT, you can learn to regulate your emotions and how you choose to express them.

Rather than fighting the reality of a situation, you can practice a deep mindfulness and techniques to better tolerate your distress. These will enable you to be able to accept situations and events better. There are many ways you can practice this. Some people count to ten, others use breathing exercises, while others still will hold an ice cube to help them focus at the moment, guiding them toward acceptance.

By using the skills taught for emotional regulation, you will be able to calmly observe and describe your emotions. This can be accomplished by solving the problem to thereby change the circumstances and your emotions, acting opposite of the way you desire or by double checking the facts of a given situation.

But before you try to influence or change your emotions using DBT, it is imperative that you first understand why these emotions are rising and where they are coming from. This is one of the main points of DBT and is one of the distinguishing factors between it and CBT. By non-judgmentally and mindfully analyzing a situation or describing your emotions, you can more effectively differentiate between fact and fiction. This will allow you to more calmly manage and control your emotions. This process is one of the reasons why DBT has been shown to be so successful in patients with anxiety and other disorders.

Depression and Suicidal Ideation

During 2002, a study was published in the American Journal of Geriatric Psychiatry. In this study, it was found that DBT is an effective therapy and treatment for depression. The results were that an astonishing seventy-one percent of the participants were free of all symptoms caused by depression by the completion of the study.

While DBT may not have been specifically created for the treatment of depression, rather it was for borderline personality disorder, it can be a significant help for those suffering from this condition. This is because the core principles and skills taught by DBT are tolerance and validation, both of which are something that people living with depression could use more of. These people often feel an overwhelming sense of loss, worthlessness, hopelessness, and sadness. Every aspect of their lives is affected and all too often they don't even want to get out of bed because that means another day living with depression will start again.

Whether or not people with depression are living in a toxic environment in which they are verbally abused or they are constantly berating themselves, circumstances in a person's life will affect their depression. However, with DBT, they can learn coping mechanisms to enable them to directly address the problems in their lives.

Journaling or the use of diary cards is another major component of DBT which can be an invaluable option for people with depression. These can help a person to better track what coping mechanisms they are using, behaviors that affect them, and their invalidating thoughts. The therapist can then look over these diary cards and help further customize the treatment process for their patient.

This will allow them to break free of their problems and stress.

It may take time, as all treatment. But studies show that when both a therapist and patient put in the work, the results will show.

Eating Disorders and Negative Body Image

Since dialectic means to have two supposedly opposite viewpoints simultaneously, this can be especially helpful for people who have eating disorders. These people often struggle with all-or-nothing thinking that is black and white. They may think that they are a complete failure and worthless if they purge one day. But if these people are able to learn to look at it with a dialectic viewpoint, then they can learn to say *"I may have purged today, but I can continue to progress and work my way through recovery."*

People who don't live with an eating disorder or other mental health condition may assume that people with these disorders are simply not trying hard enough. Yet, most people suffering from mental illness including eating disorders are giving their absolute all in order to fight against their brain and cognition. They simply haven't had access to a treatment plan that works for them.

While eating disorders are destructive and greatly weigh on a person, by following the urges of the disorder they are able to feel a small amount of relief and distraction. Thankfully, with DBT, these people can learn more beneficial ways to find the same relief and comfort but in a healthy way for both their mind and body.

The use of DBT has been increasing for people with eating disorders because of its effective focus on healthy coping mechanisms and the regulation of emotions. By learning how to identify triggers, using tools such as breathing and relaxation exercises to manage stress, and practicing mindful eating, a person can greatly improve with the use of DBT. No matter the eating disorder, this therapy has been shown to help.

While cognitive behavioral therapy has been a long used and proven method to treat eating disorders and is often best to try first if someone doesn't have success with CBT, they may want to try DBT. Experts explain how DBT can help people with eating disorders similarly to how it helps people with a borderline personality disorder who self-harm. While the conditions are different, both consist of actions that cause the person harm. Yet, these harmful actions also give the person a sense of relief from their emotional pain. This explains why helping patients learn to regulate and communicate their emotions can lead to such success with both conditions.

Chapter 6: Benefiting from CBT and DBT in Daily Life

There are many benefits to using cognitive and dialectic behavioral therapies in your daily life. You can learn to better control your emotions, process grief, make informed decisions, release stress, understand other peoples' points of view, and more.

By learning these techniques, people can find a great improvement in their lives, whether they suffer from a mental illness such as anxiety disorder, depression, an eating disorder, PTSD, OCD, or any one of a number of other conditions. But even people who are mentally healthy can learn to better understand, communicate, and control their emotions, relax, and improve their lives with these techniques.

One of the most powerful ways in which you can improve your life, whether at home, work, school, or in your social life, is by using the cognitive or ABC model. We discussed this model early on in the book and it is as simple as filling out the following:

- Situation
- Mood
- Automatic Thoughts or Images
- Evidence that Supports these Thoughts
- Evidence that Disproves these Thoughts
- Alternative Healthy Thoughts
- New Mood

Whether you choose to fill these out in a journal, on your phone, or on pre-printed sheets of paper is up to you. The important aspect is to regularly use the cognitive model when you are experiencing negative thoughts or emotions such as stress, anxiety, depression, despair, anger, jealousy, or others.

Don't treat yourself in a way that you wouldn't allow anyone else to treat you. Nobody deserves to be constantly berated and attacked. It doesn't matter if the attack is coming from an outside source or themselves.

Breathing exercises are an important tool frequently used both with CBT and DBT because they have an incredible effect on calming the mind and body that is not possible with rest. There are many different exercises you can choose from and these can be done anywhere! If you are at work, school, or a party and find yourself becoming overwhelmed or struggling with a trigger, then you can try to find a secluded place to practice these breathing techniques.

The Four Seven Eight Method

This method is simple and takes very little time, allowing it to be done anywhere. While you can use this breathing exercise in any position when you first begin learning it, practice sitting with your back straight. You will need to place the tip of your tongue directly against the tissue behind your two upper front teeth. Be sure that your tongue stays in this position for the entire breathing exercise. While performing this exercise you will be exhaling through your mouth, but if it feels awkward to be exhaling around your tongue, you can try to slightly purse your lips.

- Begin by making a whooshing sound while completely exhaling through your mouth. Then close your mouth and count to four while you quietly inhale through your nose.

- Hold your breath to the count of seven and then once again, exhale completely. Be sure that you are holding your tongue in place and that when exhaling through your mouth, you are making a whooshing sound. While you exhale count to eight.

- This process is one breath and you will want to complete it for a total of four breaths.

It is important to note that while using this technique, you want to always audibly exhale through your mouth while quietly inhaling through your nose.

The exact time you spend on each phase does not have to be four, seven, and eight seconds. But you do need to be sure to keep this ratio of numbers. If you are having a difficult time holding your breath for seven seconds, then you can simply speed up the counting so that it is still the correct ratio but does not take a full seven seconds. As you practice this breathing exercise regularly, you will be able to adjust and slow it down.

This incredible breathing technique works similarly to a tranquilizer. Yet unlike tranquilizers, this method only increases in effectiveness the more you use it. While it may be tempting to do more than a four breath rotation of this at one time, be sure that during the first month, you always take a break between each set of four breaths. After the first month, you can increase it to eight, though you may find yourself lightheaded at first.

Try to practice this technique daily, preferably at least twice a day. If you ever find yourself in an overwhelming or triggering situation, you will find yourself familiar with this technique and ability to use it to help.

Breath Counting

This method is great if you find yourself needing time to meditate and relax in the morning before work, on your lunch break, or between classes. A few minutes of breath counting will clear your mind and ease any burden you may be carrying. Even if you don't feel stressed, after completing a session of breath counting, you will be astonished by how effective it is.

- Sit somewhere comfortable with your spine straight while keeping your head slightly inclined forward. Close your eyes and take a few deep breaths. Then allow your breathing to come naturally. Don't try to influence it. Although it is ideal if the breathing is quiet and slow, the rhythm and depth may vary from person to person.

- After your breathing becomes natural, count "one" as you exhale. The next exhale, count two and continue with this pattern until you reach five.

- **After reaching five begin again at one and repeat this cycle for as long as you can. You may only complete this for three minutes, but ten minutes is preferable as this will help your mind and body reach a deeper state of relaxation.**

You will know your mind and attention have been wondering if you notice yourself counting higher than five. Simply start over at one and keep up the one to five breath cycle. You want to continue focusing on your breathing, counting, and nothing else.

If we are struggling, it can be difficult to know what to do, but with the alternative action formula, we can easily work through the problem, how to manage the effects and ways that we can cope.

- First, begin by listing any difficulties or problems you may be experiencing. Follow it with a list of your vulnerabilities regarding the situation and your known triggers that are being affected.

- After you have clearly written out your problem and understand why you are experiencing it, then you can begin to list strategies for coping. These are not solutions to the problem you have, rather it is a way you can learn to manage the effects of the temporary impact caused by the problem. After you have your list of coping strategies, list their effects and how they make you feel. You want to write down both their advantages and disadvantage in the short-term and long-term.

- Lastly, write out actions you might take instead that could possibly resolve the problem.

Whether you are struggling with OCD, an eating disorder, depression, or anxiety, by using the alternative action formula, you can easily find ways to manage your triggers and better cope. If you find that this does not help you the first time, continue giving it an effort. It may take some people a little time to find coping mechanisms that work.

The functional analysis is a popular and well-used technique within cognitive behavioral therapy. This is because it can help many people learn about themselves. If you want to know more about your specific behaviors and what they lead to, then this technique may help.

- To begin this technique, separate a piece of paper into three sections. Write out a list of any behaviors that you wish to analyze in the leftmost column. These will most often be behaviors which are potentially problematic.

- In the center column, write out any factors that may have led to the behavior in question. These factors may apply either directly or indirectly.

- On the rightmost column of the page, write out any consequences that come as a result of the behavior that you are analyzing. While "consequences" may sound inherently negative, it does not have to be that way. In fact, some of the consequences could be quite positive.

Once you have completed the functional analysis, you will have a better understanding of your behavior and whether or not it will help you attain your goals. You will find that this can help you in every aspect of your life, as it can improve both your mental health and your relationships.

We all have unhelpful and unhealthy beliefs about ourselves and our behaviors, nobody is immune from this. On one hand, we may be our own worst critic, but on the other, we can be ignorant of the ways in which we can improve. Behavior experiments are a common tool in cognitive behavioral therapy, as they get us to question our thoughts and behaviors and learn if they are truly helpful or not.

To try out this technique, decide on a behavior that you want to analyze and then commit both to using that behavior and its opposite. For instance, you may think that you are more likely to work harder and focus better if you criticize yourself.

Therefore, first test yourself and see how you work when you criticize yourself. Next, try being kind to yourself and see what you accomplish.

After you record the results of both criticizing and being kind to yourself, you can compare the two. This will give you an unbiased and honest view of whether your opinion is true or false.

Conclusion

You have learned much throughout this book, but you are not the sole person to have grown. Mary, Lydia, and Matt have all been making their own progress as well.

Mary had originally been in a constant state of depression. She was experiencing nightmares, listless during the day, unable to put her little energy into anything, distancing herself from loved ones, and frequently having thoughts such as *"Everyone is going to die and leave me behind,"* and *"What's even the point of living?"* It wasn't just painful for Mary, it was painful for everyone she cared about to see her going through such grief and unable to do anything about it.

But with the help of her psychologist, Mary learned to pick up techniques of cognitive behavioral therapy such as the cognitive model, deep breathing, functional analysis, and more. She even picked up on some dialectical behavior techniques in order to learn better acceptance of herself and her emotions.

After three months of cognitive behavioral therapy, Mary is doing much better and loving life again. She may occasionally have difficult moments, but she has learned to make use of her CBT toolkit to get her through them.

After Lydia's dream life had turned into a nightmare, she was out of options. She couldn't move away because she had signed a contract, but she was having daily overwhelming anxiety attacks. Even when she wasn't directly triggered by seeing or hearing a dog, she could begin to suddenly get anxious by just thinking about one.

After beginning therapy, she learned that she had to reduce her stress greatly. She began to do yoga, meditate, practice deep breathing, and she regularly used the cognitive model. While the change wasn't overnight, as soon as Lydia noticed she was beginning to improve, she decided to jump all the way in. She wanted to help her entire mind and body so she began eating a healthy diet, practicing better sleep hygiene, and exercising.

While exposure therapy wasn't easy at first, her therapist worked with her at her own pace so that she would feel as comfortable as possible. After beginning the process of imagining being around dogs, Lydia has finally managed to be around a large dog without having an anxiety attack. She wasn't comfortable, but she felt confident in the tools that her psychologist had provided her with. She had gained confidence by getting herself to this point.

While it was not originally easy for Matt to overcome his thoughts that therapy isn't for men, he soon learned all of the benefits it has to offer. In fact, Matt has found so much help from therapy and his psychologist that he is now a staunch supporter and recommends it regularly to people who are struggling.

It took time for Matt to become sober, but with the help of his psychologist, he learned new coping mechanisms, how to avoid triggers, and ways to manage his cravings. He even joined Alcoholics Anonymous and has made new friends there who understand his journey because they are on a similar one themselves.

Matt has also been using many techniques to control his emotions. Now, when he has anxious thoughts, rather than living in that state, he calms his mind, analyses the accuracy of the thoughts, and creates a new balanced thought. He has found this practice has also greatly improved his temper. He finds himself less often assuming people are demeaning him. And if he begins to get upset or angry, he practices breathing exercises before calmly and rationally analyzing the situation.

While the journey to change isn't an easy one, it is possible. While Matt originally thought he would only be happy with perfection, he has learned to embrace imperfection while still making progress toward his goal of a happy life free of alcohol and without uncontrollable anxiety and perfectionism.

There are many benefits to both cognitive and dialectical behavioral therapies. Whichever you choose or if you choose to combine the two, you can succeed. Whether your symptoms are mild and you are going on this journey on your own or your condition is more severe and you are using a trained professional as a guide, you can find benefit with CBT.

Even if you have previously attempted CBT and didn't improve, that doesn't mean you can't improve now. As long as you are willing to get help, be honest with yourself, and put in the effort, you can find the life you are hoping for. If you fail once, you can always try again. If you find that you aren't comfortable with a specific psychologist, then keep looking around your area until you find one that you are comfortable with. You can even find a trained psychologist or therapist to walk you through online therapy sessions.

There is no reason to continue living a life in which you are suffering or unhappy. You have access to all the tools you need to attain your dream of a happy life. Thank you for reading Cognitive Behavioral Therapy. I hope that you have learned to forgive yourself, strive forward, and find support from those around you.

Lastly, if you enjoyed this book I ask that you please take the time to review it on Audible.com. Your honest feedback would be greatly appreciated.

Thank you.

Now, I would like to share with you a free sneak peek to another one of my books that I think you will really enjoy. The book is called "Mindfulness Meditation: A Practical Guide for Beginners" Published by Barrie Muesse Scott and Mark Davenport. It's an Introduction to Learn Meditation and Become Mindful Guided Meditation, Self Hypnosis, Subliminal Affirmations, Stress Relief & Relaxation.

Enjoy!

This book is all about using the power of your thoughts to be mindful and bring peace, purpose, and happiness to your life.

Drawing upon the rich tradition of Buddhism, mindfulness meditation is all about using your thoughts to be present in the moment and crafting the world that you want to live in. If you want to be more present in your daily life, this book is for you. If you want to heal and cope with chronic diseases, this book is for you. If you want to just sleep better or deal with your depression, then this book is definitely for you. Mindfulness meditation has been shown to have extraordinary effects on your life from your mental to physical health. This book will show you how to tap into the beautiful power of mindfulness meditation no matter if you are Buddhist or not.

The following chapters will discuss everything you need to know about embracing mindfulness meditation in your day-to-day life. However, an important distinction between mindfulness and meditation needs to be made before we proceed. Oftentimes, you see mindfulness and meditation used together. Other times, you may see mindfulness and meditations used interchangeably. Meditation is the more general term that refers to the practice of fine-tuning your mind through various mental exercises. Mindfulness is a form of meditation in which one focuses on being in the very moment compared to other types of meditation practices that may use chants or mantras. For the purposes of this book, it is important to note this distinction. Any meditation practice is great! However, this book will dwell on the importance of honing in on your breath with your mindfulness meditation practice.

Mindfulness Meditation: A Practical Guide For Beginners covers five chapters. In chapter 1, mindfulness meditation will be discussed thoroughly. How key concepts in mindfulness meditation relate to Buddhism, plus the benefits of mindfulness meditation, plus answers to frequently asked questions are included. The subject of chapter 2 is about how to practice mindfulness meditation. A practical guide about which positions are best and other best practices are highlighted. Chapter 3 explores more breathing and relaxation techniques that can be used to bolster your mindfulness meditation practice. The techniques in this chapter are able to help you vary your mindfulness meditation practice. Chapter 4 is dedicated to guided mindfulness meditation exercises that can help you as you begin your meditation practice. The scrips included will help you get started so you do not have to start your meditation practice from scratch. Chapter 5 is also dedicated to guided meditations, but the mindfulness meditation scripts in this chapter focus on guided meditations designed to heal various ailments.

This book about Mindfulness and Meditation will more than prepare you to begin your journey into mindfulness and meditation. There are a lot of famous people who practice mindfulness like Naomie Harris, Boris Johnson, Katy Perry, Richard Branson, and Anderson Cooper to name a few; thus, you are in great company.

There are plenty of books on this subject on the market, so thanks again for choosing this one! Every effort was made to ensure it is full of as much useful information as possible. Please enjoy!

Chapter 1: What is Mindfulness Meditation?

> "To think in terms of either pessimism or optimism oversimplifies the truth. The problem is to see reality as it is." – Thích Nhất Hạnh

How many times have we been encouraged to see the cup half full instead of half-empty? Oftentimes in western society, the push to be optimistic and to think positive is drilled into us from a young age. However, if one is beginning to become more mindful, the transition to mindfulness may feel a little jarring as it is opposite of what feels comfortable. Imagine this. Instead of focusing just on the positive aspect of life, mindfulness encourages a realistic outlook on life that embraces the good and the bad, the positive and the negative and the neutral. And this is where our book begins, starting off by learning about this effective way of living that has been used successfully for centuries – mindfulness meditation.

Buddhist monks have been using the power of mindfulness for over 2,500 years. Mindfulness is the act of allowing your brain to rest while observing the thoughts that come and go in your mind. Mindfulness meditation is different from actively thinking and using your creative mind. When you are being mindful, you focus on an object, scene or sound that is calm and then let your thoughts gently amble by in your mind. Being mindful is powerful because if you are always caught up into being busy and always thinking about your next step, mindfulness gives you a much-needed break and makes you reflect on your pattern of thoughts and actions. It is the exact opposite of the daily living experience of most people because instead of going, mindfulness encourages you to slow down the pace.

Mindfulness allows you to know your thoughts instead of trying to change them. Instead of being judgmental and unkind to yourself if you think something negative, mindfulness has no judgment value on your thoughts. Your thoughts are just there. When you are mindful, you are taking notes of your thoughts like a note-taker. When you are in a mindful state, you just pay attention to what your thoughts are doing but giving them the freedom to do what they want. Ultimately, the goal of mindfulness is to know your mind. Once you begin to know your mind, you can begin the next step which is to train your mind.

The beautiful thing about our minds is that they are malleable, and as a result, they are trainable. Our minds are able to change based on what one is thinking. If you think the world is a horrible place, you will operate from a place of fear and your actions will show that. If you think that the world is a wonderful place, you will operate from a place of reckless optimism without being able to be realistic about certain dangers you may find yourself in. Mindfulness helps you to know your thoughts and then begin to train your thoughts to become more in tune with your long-term goals. Mindfulness slows down the grind of your busy daily pace and gives you a different vantage point about patterns in your life. These patterns can be feelings that you have in certain situations or your reactions to how other people treat you. When you are being mindful, you may notice trends and patterns that you are constantly thinking. Are you always wanting more and more? Do you feel comfortable with the way things are? Whatever patterns you notice, mindfulness can help you pinpoint what types of things are causing you mental, anguish, conflict, or joy. Then after noticing these patterns, you can begin to shape it to how you would like to be by focusing on being more gracious, compassionate, and kind with your thoughts.

When you begin your practice, do not treat your mindfulness meditation practices as an obligatory item on your daily to-do list. When you meditate, you want to be present in the moment, not treating the practice as an aggressive measuring stick to how fast you can change or using your meditation practice as a form of escapism without being willing to change your ideals. The most important thing to remember before you begin is that you are training your mind to be at peace with how things are going in the world, no matter what is happening. Once you are able to be at peace in no matter what situation you find yourself in, then you are able to start to work on yourself to change your values. Mindfulness meditation is not a sprint; it is a marathon that you continually work on until you are finally able to free yourself from unsavory emotions that are clinging to you whether they are anger, agitation, negativity, self-image issues, unfair, hasty judgments, and biased opinions and ideals.

When you are training your mind to be more mindful, affirmations are great tools to use. Affirmations are very helpful, especially when you create them yourself. The thought process behind using affirmations is to use very direct language which influences your subconscious to help you get the outcome that you want to get. When you use affirmations, you want to first figure out what outcome it is that you want. Then create a short sentence with an active word. Make sure the sentence is in the present tense. For example, if you want to feel calmer and not be so anxiety-ridden, you can create an affirmation to help. You will start with the outcome of being calmer and make that into a statement using the present tense. Thus, the affirmation would be 'I am more calm.' By using the present tense, you are affirming the future outcome. When the affirmation is created, you can say it during your meditation time and throughout the day. When you couple this practice of saying affirmations with your mindfulness meditation session, they work doubly together to help you get the outcome that you want to get. For example, you hear the term think positive all the time. It is because positive thinking can help shape your future to where you have a positive future. However, if you think negative oftentimes a reality reflects your thoughts. Our thoughts influence our subconscious which in turn can determine our reality.

Mindfulness meditation helps you shape your reality by taking the time to know your mind. Once you know your mind, you will be able to train it and ultimately free it from negative, debilitating thinking. Every step works together. Before you begin your mindfulness meditation practice, know that it is not going to be easy. It will be a journey, but if you are dedicated, you will see a difference in your life.

The History of Mindfulness Meditation

For Buddhists, nurturing mindfulness is the ultimate path to enlightenment. The point of Buddhism is to reach the highest truth by focusing on overcoming the limitations that your body has. Buddhists practice mindfulness by using four foundational truths of mindfulness. The four truths originate from a Buddhist sutta or sutra which is similar to a form of Buddhist scripture. The name of the sutta is called "The Discourse on the Establishing of Mindfulness" or the *Satipatthana sutta*. Please remember that the four establishments of mindfulness come from a very long and rich history. This book cannot possibly cover everything related to them, but hopes to serve as a general overview that can deepen your understanding of mindfulness meditation. The four truths are mindfulness of the body, mindfulness of feelings, mindfulness of consciousness and mindfulness of phenomena. Each foundation normally goes step-by-step in a flowing manner. You can go in and out of meditating upon each truth. They all work together. The first stop on the mindfulness journey is mindfulness of the body.

What is the one thing that you typically hear before beginning any form of meditation? The answer is watching your breath. Most meditation practices or guided meditations instruct you to begin by taking deep breaths in and exhaling deep breaths. Therefore, when you practice mindfulness, the first step is to think about mindfulness of your body. Initially, you'll want to start by being mindful of your breathing. Notice how deep or how shorts your breaths are when you start your meditation session. There are also different forms of body mindfulness you can focus on as well, such as mindfulness of eating or mindfulness of how you walk. These are some of the easiest mindfulness of the body to begin with, but we will focus on mindfulness of breathing since breathing is key to healing lots of ailments, physical and mental in your body.

Mindfulness of the body is just not about the positions your body is sitting in or how you breathe, eat and walk. Mindfulness of the body also involves a deeper understanding of how all your body parts work together. This includes how your leg connects to your thigh, how your ears function, or the power of body working throughout your body. Mindfulness of the body also seeks to understand some of the more unpleasant bodily functions such as urine or snot boogers or blood. The purpose of being mindful of your body is to reflect on how your body functions. You may ask, how do I try to be mindful of my body when I am meditating? An easy introductory way to do this is to imagine yourself greeting and thanking each body part for what it does. You can start at your feet and work your way up until you reach the top of your body.

The next foundation you should be concerned with when practicing mindfulness meditation is mindfulness of your feelings. A better way to explain mindfulness of your feelings is that this truth is concerned about being mindful of your neutral, painful, and pleasurable feelings. You can also reflect on how to be mindful of these feelings by using the senses of your touch, smell, hearing, seeing, taste, and your mind. In Buddhism, your mind is considered a sixth sense. It important to be mindful of these feelings because when you have painful feelings they can lead to fear and hatred. Too many neutral feelings can cause you to become disinterested and floated through life. When you are neutral about something, you are not concerned about it and as a result, it will not be important to you. Lastly, you have to be mindful of pleasurable feelings because too many pleasurable feelings can lead to lust and greed. It is important to be non-judgmental and only observe your thoughts, not acknowledge them when you meditate. The reason you do not want to acknowledge anything is that once you begin to acknowledge a thought as a neutral, painful or pleasurable feeling, you are in danger of attaching yourself to feelings that will prevent you from being enlightened. Thus, it is best to use mindfulness to observe when you are gaining feelings of neutrality, pleasure or painful so you know how to handle those feelings appropriately. When you practice mindfulness of feelings, you will still experience feelings.

Mindfulness of feelings does not mean that you do not feel. It only means that you are able to enjoy the feelings without going overboard to the point of the feelings cause you to become obsessed and overly attached to the thing that is causing the feeling, whether those feelings are good or bad. For example, if you love doughnuts and you find yourself obsessing over doughnuts, you can enjoy them so much that you want more and more doughnuts because of the pleasurable feeling that doughnuts give you. Eating too many doughnuts can cause issues your health like diabetes or chronic inflammation. All of these feelings started because of the seemingly innocent, yet pleasurable feeling of liking doughnuts. On the other side, if you are leery of a certain political leaning and it brings you immense pleasure, attaching yourself to that displeasure can quickly lead to hatred and biased feelings. However, if you are able to know your thoughts and know that this political leaning causes displeasure, you can work to be mindful that the political leaning is a trigger for you without attaching too much to that feeling to the point that it goes overboard. Likewise, if you feel neutral about a person, you can become so disinterested in them that you lose focus of the fact that they are human and worthy of respect. Hence, if they ever needed something, you would most likely overlook them or drag your feet to help them. So even feelings of neutrality can be dangerous. Once you become too attached to any type of feeling, the excess doting on the feeling prevents you from reaching enlightenment.

The next foundation of mindfulness meditation that you want to build upon is mindfulness of your consciousness. In Buddhism, there are 52 mental formations. Mental formations translated loosely are emotions and states of mind. The mental formations are normally grouped together in a specific way. The first of these formations are the previous feelings that were discussed in the mindfulness of feelings consisting of feelings of pleasure, neutrality, and displeasure. The next 51 formations are what the mindfulness of the consciousness helps you to focus on that are clustered in different groups. These include:

- Proficiency of mental properties
- Pliancy of mental properties
- Perception
- Composure of mind
- Appreciation
- Effort
- Righteousness of mind
- Worry
- Desire to do
- Amity
- Psychic life
- Error
- Perplexity
- Feeling
- Right livelihood
- Volition
- Initial application
- Attention
- Greed
- Buoyancy of mental properties
- Adaptability of mind
- Recklessness
- Right speech
- Sloth
- Discretion
- Proficiency of mind
- Modesty
- Conceit
- Right action
- Faith
- Buoyancy of mind

- Pliancy of mind
- Contact
- Deciding
- Concentration of mind
- Torpor
- Mindfulness
- Disinterestedness
- Envy
- Shamelessness
- Adaptability of mental properties
- Distraction
- Composure of mental properties
- Dullness
- Balance of mind
- Sustained application
- Pity
- Selfishness
- Reason
- Righteousness of mental properties
- Hate

This is a general overview of the mental formations, but you can study them in more detail to get a more detailed understanding. To simplify this foundation, when you are practicing mindfulness of the conscience, be observant of the different feelings that go in and out of your brain. To easily start meditating with mindfulness of the conscience, when you meditate observe any thoughts that you have. When your mind drifts from focusing on your breathing, you can call out to yourself that you are being mindful. When your mind begins to drift from not meditating, you can call out to yourself that you are not being mindful. This simple exercise is using mindful of your consciousness. It is also a great trick to use in your everyday life when you want to be more mindful.

The last foundation of mindfulness that you want to build upon is mindfulness of phenomena or mindfulness of perception. When you think of a car, you know it is an object that has four wheels and has the capacity to take you here and there. The idea that you have in your mind of a car may be realistic and based on a car that you know personally. Or the idea of a car that you may have can be based on what your perception of what a car is generally, according to your knowledge of what a car is. When you practice mindfulness of mental objects, you try to focus on the 'why' of how you perceive something. If you think of cars as positive, this positive association could be because of a childhood memory that when growing up you had a wonderful experience of your parents taking you to school every day in an old beat up, yet comfortable car. If you have a negative perception of cars, it could be because your friend was killed by a car or cars cause you to think of all the damage that they do to the ozone layer. Mindfulness of perception allows you to focus on the experiences that shape your perception of what something is so you can bypass those perceptions to get to the true meaning of what something actually is and not what you think something is.

When you practice mindfulness of perception, you want to be aware of things that can cause your perception to be tainted. These can be known as the 5 hindrances. You also want to be mindful of the 7 factors of awakening which should be what you aspire your perceptions to be based on. When all of these factors work together, it helps you eliminate suffering. The 7 factors of awakening that you want to focus on when you practice mindfulness of perception include:

- Equanimity – This factor can be described as the calm observance of things around you.
- Energy – This is the energy that powers you to lead the investigation to seek understanding about different

topics in life.
- Concentration – The complete focus of the mind is what this factor seeks.
- Investigation of your perception – This factor encourages you to seek knowledge about phenomena to understand how something operates.
- Joy -Balanced pleasurable interest in something is what this factor is all about.
- Tranquility – Serenity and quietness encompass this factor.
- Mindfulness – Present moment awareness describes this factor.

The 5 hindrances to avoid are:
- Dullness – Doing your takes half-heartedly with no vim or lacking concentration.
- Lust – A craving for pleasure to fulfill all your senses.
- Ill will – Feelings of hatred directed to others.
- Restlessness and worry – This is when you are unable to calm your mind.
- Doubt – A lack of trust or conviction.

When you monitor your thoughts to see if any of the 5 hindrances appear in your train of thoughts, you want to note when and why they arose. You'll also want to note how you can prevent the hindrance from appearing again and how you can replace the hindrance with one of the 7 factors of awakening in their wake.

As you work on your mindfulness meditation, strive to attain the four foundational truths in the order of mindfulness of body, mindfulness of feelings, mindfulness of consciousness, and mindfulness of perception. This is ideal. However, you can meditate upon all of the foundations in one setting as well. So, if you focus on more than one truth at a time, that is ok as well. To truly attain enlightenment, you must find a way to master them all.

Lastly, mindfulness meditation helps you cultivate awareness of the "three characteristics of experience." According to Buddhism, if you do not understand these three characteristics, then you are bound to be caught up into an endless cycle of suffering. The three characteristics you should be aware of are the traits of impermanence, or *anitya*, dissatisfaction, or *duhkha*, and egolessness, or *anatma*. Impermanence means that all conditioned things will change. There is a constant change that you must be aware of. The next trait of dissatisfaction means that there is pain and suffering and no satisfaction in an unenlightened state. *Anatma* means that one should strive to act without an ego. These three are another aspect of Buddhist underpinnings behind the mindfulness meditation practice. These are great to keep in the back up your mind when you are doing mindfulness meditation.

Hopefully, up until this point, the case for why you practice mindfulness has been made. In case you still are not convinced, let's try to convince you one more time. So why mindfulness? There are lots of different meditation practices you can choose from, but mindfulness meditation is a great way to begin for a few different reasons.

Mindfulness is awesome because it:
- Helps you not be judgmental – One of the major components of mindfulness is to not be judgmental of yourself and others. This gentleness towards yourself improves your overall self-esteem. It also encourages self-compassion for yourself and for others.
- Easy and fast – There is no set time to do it. It is super

easy to pick up on and relatively fast to do. Your sessions can be as long as they need to be or as short as they can be. If you have a busy schedule, you can meditate for 5 minutes or however long is best for you.

- Reduces stress instantly -Because the necessity of breathing is at the core of mindfulness meditation, deep breathing immediately reduces the stress you may be feeling as soon as you begin your mindfulness meditation session.
- Improves your wisdom – Mindfulness meditation improves your wisdom because you are able to figure out what makes you tick by noting and understanding the power of your thoughts. You also are able to be wise about other people, because this system meditation improves your observation skills such that you will be able to observe others and make connections about their behavior in ways that you have not been able to before.
- No set way to do it – For some people, the fact there is no set structure may be limiting to them, but it is a positive because there is not a right or wrong way to do it.
- Relaxing and calms your nerves – Just like reducing your stress instantly, mindfulness meditation also relaxes and calms your nerves due to the power of breathing.
- Observe yourself in the moment – Mindfulness meditation allows you to be in tune with your thoughts and actions so you are able to get into the 'zone' a lot easier than before.
- Easy to pick-up – Did I mention how easy mindfulness meditation is to pick up? Once you have one session, you will be able to do more rather easily.
- Doesn't have to depend on anyone else to do it – Mindfulness meditation is great to practice on your own.

So you never have to worry about if the teacher is going to show up to class or not. This meditation style is self-guided so you can set your schedule according to your convenience.

Thank you, this preview is now over.

I hope you enjoyed this preview of my book Mindfulness Meditation: A Practical Guide for Beginners - An Introduction to: Guided Meditation, Self Hypnosis, Subliminal Affirmations, Stress Relief & Relaxation. Learn to Meditate and Become Mindful" by Barrie Muesse Scott and Mark Davenport. Please make sure to check out the full book on Amazon.com

Thank you.

www.ingramcontent.com/pod-product-compliance
Lightning Source LLC
Chambersburg PA
CBHW020122130526
44591CB00032B/347